THE BASICS OF BIT BLOCKCHAIN 2021

Basics of Cryptocurrency for the Beginners

Disclaimer Notice

Warning

There is no magic formula of getting rich overnight in the financial market or anywhere else. Investing in this market could cost you a lot of money. By reading the book you will get to know the risks and strategies of investing in the cryptocurrency market. The book won't be accountable for any kinds of financial loss.

Table of Contents:

Chapter 1

Hard Money vs Digital Money

How do we define money?

Money is a unit that acts as a generally recognized means of exchange for transactional purposes in an economy. It is usually referred to as currency. The use of money provides a medium for buying and selling in a market. Money is a source in the form of a product, having a physical property to be adopted by market users as a means of exchange. Money facilitates us by the service of reducing transaction costs, especially the double coincidence of wants. The double coincidence of wants is a global problem in a barter system. When people trade with each other, the first party must have something to sell that the other party wants to buy.

Early forms of bartering do not provide the facility of divisibility. For instance, if a person has cows but needs bananas, he must find a person who has bananas and the need for meat. What if that person finds someone who has the demand for meat but no bananas and can only offer shoes? To get root, that individual must find a person who has bananas and wants shoes, and so on.

The lack of transferability of bartering for items is complicated, confusing, and inefficient. But that is not where the end of the problem; even if the person meets someone to sell meat for bananas, they may not think many bananas are worth a whole cow. This type of trade requires an agreement and original way to decide how many bananas are worth some cow parts. Money solved these problems. It meant that money was a precious commodity in itself, such as cattle in earliest civilizations, later gold and silver by weight, and finally coinage – gold and silver coins. Money only has value as a means of exchange because the people accept it and is legally enforced by the government acting on behalf and benefit of the people.

Characteristics of Money

According to economists, money has four basic characteristics

1. Means of Payment.

2. Unit of Account.

3. Store of Value.

Properties of Money

As money is most valuable, a currency should have these properties:

1)Fungible, 2) Durable, 3) Portable, 4) Recognizable, and 5) Stable.

Fungible

Units of the product should be of relatively equitable quality so that they are exchangeable with each other. The different divisions of the goods also have additional attributes. The value for use in future transactions may not be definitive or consistent. Money is used as non-fungible good results in transaction costs of separately estimating units before an exchange can occur.

Durable

The item's physical properties should be durable enough to continue its value in future exchanges and can be used multiple times. A good that devalues quickly with use will not be helpful for future transactions trying to use money as a non-durable reasonable disagreement with money's necessarily future-oriented value.

Portable

The money should be divisible into small proportions so that people appreciate its actual value. A beneficial quantity of the good can be carried or transported conveniently. An indivisible item or item of low real use-value may create issues. A high transaction cost produces when trying to use a non-portable good as money. Either physically transporting vast quantities of the standard value items or defining practical, transferable possession of an indivisible or unmoving object.

Recognizable

The originality and quantity of the good should be readily acceptable to the users to determine the terms of the exchange quickly. People trying to use an unidentifiable good as money by all the parties at the time of sale produces transaction costs of agreement on the reliability and quantity of the goods

Stable

The value should be increasing or remain constant over time that people agree on a good or item in charge of the other goods they will trade. An object whose value changes widely up and down over time or decreases consistently is not very suitable. Trying to use a conflicting interest as money produces transaction costs of frequently revaluing the good in each running transaction. The risk is that the exchange value of the item might decrease its other direct use-value or not be helpful at all. Money will no circulate for an extended period in this case.

A brief history of money.

Money for at least the last 3,000 years has been part of human history in some way, shape, or form. Before that time, historians agree that it was likely a used system. Goods and services trade among people indirectly is possible through money. They can communicate the prices of goods they want and provide a way to store their wealth.

Around 770 B.C., the Chinese moved from actual objects that are usable, such as tools and weapons, for trading as a medium of exchange. To using miniature replicas of these objects that had been diffuse in bronze. Due to lack of awareness, most people have conflicts on these items for trading. Then these tiny daggers, spades, and hoes were eventually scarce for objects in the shape of a circle. These objects then became the first coins.

For the first time, China used coins as an object that modern people recognize. The first region of the world was Europe to use an industrial facility to manufacture coins that could be used as currency in Lydia (now western Turkey). The process of creating money in this way is called minting.

Lydia's King Alyattes minted the first official currency in 600 B.C. The coins were made from a combination of silver and gold called electrum, which occurs naturally. The coins were denominated with pictures. In the streets of Sardis, in 600 B.C., Lydia's currency helped the country increase both its internal and external trading systems, making it one of the wealthiest empires in Asia Minor.

Around 700 B.C., the Chinese moved to paper money. Marco Polo was a Venetian merchant, writer, and explorer who traveled through Asia along the Silk Road between A.D. 1271 and 1295. Visited China in approximately A.D. 1271, the emperor of China had reasonable control on both the various denominations and money supply.

Europe was still using metal coins as their only form of currency in different parts of Europe up to the 16th century. Colonial efforts helped them;

European conquest allowed them to acquire new territories. With new sources of precious metals and authorized them to keep minting a vast quantity of coins.

However, for depositors and borrowers, banks eventually started using paper banknotes to transfer in place of metal coins. These notes were exchanged and could be taken to the bank for their face value in metal–commonly silver or gold–coins. This paper money could use to buy and sell goods and services. In this way, it utilizes much like currency does today in the modern world. However, the issue was which is now responsible for issuing currency in most countries by banks and private institutions, not the government,

Colonial governments in North America issued the first paper currency issued by European governments. Because shipments took so long between Europe and the North American colonies, the colonists frequently ran out of cash as an enlarged operation. The colonial governments issued IOUs traded as a currency instead of going back to a barter system; the first instance was Canada. In 1685, France soldiers were given playing cards denominated and signed by the governor to use cash instead of coins.

The 21st century has given a surge to two forms of currency: mobile payments and virtual currency. Mobile payments are money provided for a product or service through a moveable electronic device, such as a cell phone, smartphone, or tablet device. Can also be used mobile payment technology to send money to friends or family members. Increasingly, services like Apple Pay and Google Pay are platforms for point-of-sale payments for the users.

Forms of Money

There were four different types of money throughout history is not surprising. To give a brief overview, take a look at the four most relevant ones below: (1) commodity money, (2) fiat money, (3) fiduciary money, and (4) commercial bank money.

Commodity Money

Most likely, the oldest and most straightforward type of money is commodity money. It is closely related to (and derived from) a barter system; goods and services are directly exchanged for other goods and services in this system. Because commodity money overall acts as a medium of exchange, so it facilitates this process. The critical thing about commodity money is that its value is determined by the intrinsic value of the commodity itself. In other words, we can say, the item itself becomes money. Examples of commodity money include metal coins, beads, shells, spices, weapons, etc.

Fiat Money

Fiat (means order or command) money gets its value from a government order. The government declares fiat money as legal tenders, essential for all people and firms to accept payment sources. Fiat money can't be backed by any physical or material commodity, unlike commodity money. The intrinsic value of fiat money is significantly lower than its face value. Hence, the value of fiat money is got from the relationship between supply and demand. Examples of fiat money include bills and coins.

Fiduciary Money

The value of fiduciary money depends on the confidence that it will be generally accepted as a means of exchange. Unlike fiat money, it is not declared legal tender by the government, which means people are not restricted by law to trust it as a means of payment. If the bearer requests it, the issuer of fiduciary money promises to return for a commodity or fiat money. As long as fiduciary money becomes authentic, people are confident that this promise will not break. They start using fiduciary money just like regular fiat or commodity money. Examples of fiduciary money include cheques, banknotes, or drafts.

Commercial Bank Money

Commercial bank money can be defined as claims against financial institutions like banks used to purchase goods or services. It represents the part of a currency that is made of debt generated by commercial banks. Commercial bank money is created through what we call fractional reserve banking. Commercial banks give out loan worth more than the value of the actual currency they hold, which is called fractional reserve banking. At this point, just note that, in essence, commercial bank money is debt generated so that it can be exchanged for "real" money or to buy goods and services.

Physical Money and Digital Money

Physical Money and Digital Money

Physical Money

The English word "cash" means "money box" and later came to have a secondary meaning, "money". In the 18th century, this secondary usage became the sole meaning.

The physical notes plus coins exist in the smallest number to convey accounts information outside the banks' secure networks. In other words, banks are simply durable, agreeably specific communications devices, carrying accounts information hand-to-hand across the economy. Physical money is made with no intrinsic value; you could not get anything for the paper or base metals from which they are made. Because the purpose only exists to carry information. You could liken money to any other legal agreement that might be recorded on paper; The value lies in the knowledge or understanding it memorializes, not in the document on which a contract is signed no intrinsic value,

Cash has now become a tiny part of the money supply. Its remaining role is to provide currency storage and payment for those who do not want to take part in other payment systems and make small payments easily and quickly. However, this latter role is being replaced more frequently by digital money. Research has found that as debit card usage increases, the demand for cash decreases because traders need to make fewer customer purchases.

Physical Money Advantages

Several advantages a cashless society has:

- The possibility of accepting counterfeit money reduces for the payments that are not completed. It reduces the costs of a business and
- risks
- . In addition, a company is not exposed to theft, burglary, or robbery of cash. Furthermore, as the number of cashless payments increases, the costs of processing and securing money will also reduce.
- Transaction speed increased. According to a study the Restaurant chain Sweetgreen conducted, it can complete a cashless transaction on average 15% faster than a cash transaction.
- In a cashless society funding illegal activities, illegal transactions, tax fraud, and money laundering are more challenging to execute. Criminal

activities decrease by the elimination of high-denomination bills. It is easier to detect more extensive amounts of cash carry by criminals and making it harder to transport.

- A cashless society comes up with more straightforward consumer budgeting. All transactions are saved that are completed in digital payments, and they are easily reachable to any customer. This information is used to assist anyone in reading just their budget more efficiently.

- The transmission of disease through coins and banknotes is avoided when cash is not using.

Physical Money Disadvantages

On the other hand, a cashless economy also has some disadvantages:

- Privacy becomes an issue in the digital world. In a cashless economy, all payments and transactions are traceable. In this type of economy, business organizations utilize customer information to forecast future transactions and, based on their spending habits, create consumer profiles; this information is available to the government. A data breach can also be destructive to any consumer, allowing criminals to use this information for their purposes.
- A cashless society creates a problem for the unbanked. There are various groups of the population in a community, such as children, the elderly, and poor people, who are entirely dependent on cash. A consumer must know a certain level of digital payment and a bank account in a cashless society. Overspending is a serious concern in a cashless society. When using a debit or credit card it is much easier for anyone to lose track of how much money is spent

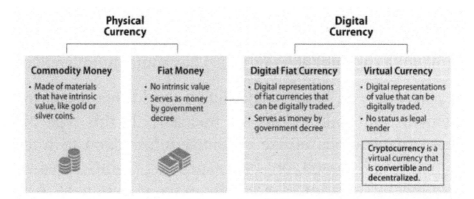

Digital Money

Digital currency is a form of currency that's available exclusively in electronic form. Electronic money already predominates most countries' financial systems. In the U.S., about <u>one-tenth of the overall money supply</u> is in the circulation of the physical U.S. currency. The remainder is held in electronic form in various bank deposits.

What differentiates digital currency from electronic money currently in most Americans' bank accounts never takes physical form. Digital currency, whatever, never takes physical form. It remains on a computer network and is always exchanged via digital means.

For example, using your mobile device, you'd make purchases by transferring digital currency to retailers instead of using physical dollar bills.

Following are the successful <u>cryptocurrencies</u> like <u>Bitcoin</u> and <u>Ethereum</u>, which any central authorities, governments do not manage, and central banks worldwide. They are researching the possibility of creating their digital currencies, commonly known as central bank digital currencies.

Digital Money Advantages

- Through digital currency, payments are completed much faster than current means, like ACH or wire transfers, which can take days to confirm a transaction. For financial institutions.
- International currency transactions are costly; when it involves currency conversions individuals are charged high fees to move funds from one country to another.

- Existing money transfers often take more time because banks are closed during weekends and outside regular business hours can't confirm transactions. With digital currency, it is possible transactions work at the same speed 24 hours a day, seven days a week.
- The government sends payments like tax refunds, child benefits and food stamps to people immediately. If developing a CBDC, it could, rather than mail them a check or figure out prepaid debit cards.

Digital Money Disadvantages

- The current popularity of cryptocurrency is a downside. "Across different blockchains there are so many digital currencies being created that all have their limitations. It will time taking to determine which digital currencies may be applicable for some instances.
- It is the disadvantage of digital currencies that they require work for the user to learn how to perform fundamental tasks, like how to open and use a digital wallet and properly store digital asset. For digital currencies the system needs to get simpler to access them quickly and securely.
- computers must solve complicated equations to verify and record transactions where cryptocurrencies use the blockchain,
- . It takes considerable electricity, and blockchain transactions get more expensive as there are more transactions. However, these would probably not exist for a CBDC since the central bank would likely control it. The complex consensus processes are not needed.
- Digital currency prices and values can change suddenly. Cunha believes this is why people are resisting using it as a medium of exchange. "What if I hold a Bitcoin just for a week, and it loses 20% of value? As a business, do I want to accept something that unstable?" With CBDC, although the value is much stabler cannot fluctuate, like paper currency.
- A U.S. CBDC is still hypothetical and will take time. If the government decides to produce one, there will be costs associated with its development.

Money Through the Ages

The history of money supports the development of economic and social systems that give at least one of the functions of money. These systems can be understood as means of trading wealth indirectly, not directly as with barter. Money facilitates this process of trading.

Money may take a physical form as notes and coins or may exist as an electronic or written account. It may have the intrinsic value be legally exchangeable for something with inherent value (representative money) or only have a nominal value (fiat money)

Due to the complexities of ancient history (as earliest civilizations evolve at different paces and not keeping accurate records or having their records destroyed). So that it is impossible to find the exact origin of the invention of money and move from "barter systems" to the "monetary systems". Further, evidence in history supports the idea that money has taken two primary forms of account (debits and credits on ledgers) and cash of exchange (tangible media of exchange made from clay, leather, paper, bamboo, metal, etc.).

Respecting money of exchange, the use of representative money historically pre-dates the invention of coinage as well. In the ancient empires of Egypt, India, Babylon, and China, the temples and famous palaces often had commodities. Warehouses that used clay tokens and other materials for trading may serve as evidence of a claim upon a portion of the goods stored in the warehouses. These tokens could be redeemed easily at the warehouse for the commodity they represented. They could be traded in the markets as if they had the entity or given to workers as payment. Throughout history, gold and silver have been the most common forms of money. In many languages, such as French, Hebrew, Spanish, and Italian, silver is still related to the word for money. Sometimes other metals were used. For instance, Ancient Sparta discourages its citizens from engaging in foreign trade minted coins from iron. Sweden lacked precious metals in the early 17th century. It produced "plate money": large slabs of copper 50 cm or more in length and width, stamped with indications of their value.

From about 1000 BC, money was in the form of spades, and small knives made of bronze were in use in China during the Zhou dynasty; before this, they used cast bronze replicas of cowrie shells.

Around the Aegean Sea 7th century B.C., the first manufactured actual coins appear separately in India, China, and other cities. In Song dynasty China, paper money was first introduced during the 11th century. In the seventh century, the development of the banknote started with local issues of paper currency. Its roots were in trader or merchant of deposit during the Tang dynasty (618–907). Traders and wholesalers want to avoid the heavy quantity of large commercial buying and selling transactions.

Mughal Empire continues its use in the economy as money. 3rd century B.C., the history of the rupee traces back to Ancient India circa Ancient India was one of the earliest issuers of coins globally, along with the Lydian staters, several other Middle Eastern coinages, and the Chinese wen. In the Indian subcontinent (1540–1545), Sher Shah Suri, for the first time, introduced a silver coin called a rupiya, weighing 178 grams. The term from rūpya, a Sanskrit term for silver coin, from Sanskrit rūpa, is a beautiful form.

The imperial taka was officially introduced in 1329 by the monetary reforms of Muhammad bin Tughluq. It was modeled as indicative money, a concept introduces as paper money by the Mongols in China and Persia. The taka was minted in brass and copper, exchanged its value with reserves of gold and silver in the imperial treasury. This type of currency was introduced due to the shortage of metals.

Paper money became known in Europe, in the 13th century, through travelers' accounts, such as Marco Polo and William of Rubruck. In Italy and Flanders, money traders started using promissory notes. Because of the impracticality and insecurity of transporting large sums of money over long distances. In the beginning these promissory notes were personally registered. Still, they soon became a written order to pay the amount to whoever had it in their possession. These notes can be used as a predecessor to regular banknotes.

Stockholms Banco was the first European banknotes issued by a predecessor of Sweden's central bank Sveriges Riksbank, in 1661. These banknotes replaced the copper plates as a means of payment, although in 1664, the bank ran out of coins to redeem notes and end up operating in the same year.

In the late 20th century, debit cards and credit cards became the most accessible means of payment in the First World. The Bankamericard was launched in 1958; it became the first third-party credit card used and accepted in shops and stores all over the United States, soon followed by the Mastercard and the American Express.

In the second part of the 20th century, the development of computer technology allowed money to be represented digitally. In 1990, in the United States, it transferred all money electronically between its central bank and commercial banks. By the 2000s, most money existed in banks databases as a digital currency. In 2012, by several transactions, 20 to 58 percent of transactions were electronic (dependent on country). The primary benefit of digital money is that it allows payments for more accessible, cheaper, faster, and more flexible.

In 2008, Bitcoin was presented by an unknown author under the pseudonym of Satoshi Nakamoto. Its use of cryptography enabled the currency to have a fungible, trustless, and tamper-resistant distributed ledger called a blockchain. It became the first broadly used decentralized, peer-to-peer, currency. Since the 1980s, other comparable systems had been proposed. The protocol proposed by Satoshi Nakamoto solved what is known as the double-spending problem without the need for a trusted third-party.

Since Bitcoin originated, thousands of cryptocurrencies have been introduced, for example, dogecoin, etherium, litecoin, etc.

Inter Bank Payment System

The interbank payment system transfers funds from the payer's bank to the beneficiary's bank. Banks and the other payers of payment services carry out the payments based on their client's instructions. Transfer in the form of a written document (payment instruction forms. direct debit forms, etc.), or by technical means (via internet banking, vocally by phone, or via special banking applications by mobile phone, or using a payment card. which may also consider an electronic payment instruction).

Suppose the payer and the payee have their accounts at the same bank. In that case, they will perform the money transfer (account settlement) in its clearing center. Suppose both parties have accounts with different banks. In that case, the payer's bank only has to use the "interbank clearing center" to transfer money.

There are two steps clearing and settlement to processing funds transfers. The clearing is transferring and verifying information between the payer (sending financial institution) and the payee (receiving financial institution). Settlement is the actual transfer process of funds between the payer's financial institution and the payee's financial institution. The settlement releases the responsibility of the payer financial institution to the payee financial institution concerning the payment order. The final settlement is irreversible and unconditional. The payment is determined finally by that system's rules and applicable law.

Payment messages generally may be credit transfers or debit transfers. Most credit transfer systems are used for large-value fund transfers. Both payment messages and funds move from the payer financial institution to the payee financial institution. An institution transmits a payment order (a message that requests funds transfer to the payee) to start a funds transfer. Typically necessary to process the payment orders, large-value payment system operating procedures include identification, reconciliation, and confirmation procedures. Financial institutions contract with one or more third parties to help perform clearing and settlement activities.

The legal framework for institutions offering payment services is complex. There are rules for large-value payments that are complex and definite from retail prices. Large-value funds transfer (LFT) systems differ from retail electronic funds transfer (EFT) systems. Which generally operate a large volume of low-value payments, including automated clearing house (ACH) and debit and credit card transactions at the point of sale.

International Payment System

International payments are transactions that involve only banks, also known as cross-border payments or global payments. International payment systems work as a bridge between companies, individuals, banks, and settlement institutions operating in at least two different countries with different currencies that need to be paid.

However, when we discuss in detail, international payments make our economy succeed. According to the U.S. Treasury, SWIFT (a send and receive agent for international fees) operate about $5 trillion per day. Given that SWIFT performs, approximately $1.25 quadrillion dollars is transferred globally every year.

What are some practices for cost-effective international payments?

Dual invoicing

Pay in local funds eliminating buffers traders or vendors add for rate fluctuation. International traders usually add a risk margin to account for potential adverse rate movements on the U.S. dollar (USD), which can cost your business. They not only have to account for the change in currency value, but they must plan for the rate at which their bank is going to convert the funds from USD into their local currency.

To cover foreign exchange, paying in USD to foreign suppliers can increase 15 percent in total costs. To save the most with international payments paying in local funds by receiving a dual invoice is considered one of the most cost-effective and efficient ways.

Flexible payments

Flexibility is vital when a corporation wants to convert its funds back to its currency send money around the world. A payment policy sets the framework exactly when using a low-cost method like Global EFT is the correct payment method. Sending a wire is necessary if speed is the highest priority.

If a corporation adopts an effective payment policy also helps businesses to create stable budgets so cash flow, pricing, and revenue forecasting can be accurate. Using F.X. hedging tools to minimize the effect of inconstancy reduces uncertainty which all businesses can appreciate.

Account analysis

Uncover fees and markups being applied to your foreign exchange current payments. In one study, only 38% of respondents said when sending cross-border payments; they believe they are getting a competitive foreign exchange rate. Most still stay unaware and continue to pay high rates and fees than necessary.

Using recent payment history, a payments analyst can easily calculate the costs and available savings that can immediately impact business.

Liquidity provider

Seamlessly transfer cross-currency funds between accounts with lower rates and fees. Liquidity can make a big difference, whether it transfer funds from other countries. Moving funds from a receivables account to operating accounts or funding business units outside your home country. Make sure to use a supplier that offers fast clearing options so you can use the funds as soon as possible while ensuring your rates are still competitive.

Many businesses don't perceive the additional conversion costs of using the bank they have their accounts with instead of specialists.

Different E-Money Wallets

A digital wallet is an electronic device, software, or online service that enables traders or businesses to make transactions electronically. A digital wallet is known as an e-wallet. It stores the payment information on various users' websites for different payment modes through other items such as gift coupons and driver's licenses.

A digital wallet can exist in different forms, such as a desktop or in the form of a smartphone. However, mobile apps are the most popular and convenient version of the digital wallet, owing to their mobility and flexibility. Digital wallets are not only suitable to use in some instances but also safer than traditional wallets. To avail of the service, users of digital wallets need to download the particular apps created by banks or trusted third parties.

Types of Digital Wallets

The following are the types of digital wallets:

1. Closed Wallet

A company selling products or services can develop a closed wallet for customers. Users of a secured wallet can use the funds stored to make payments or transactions only with the issuer of the wallet. In case of cancellations, returns, or refunds, money is stored in the wallets. Amazon Pay is an example of the most reliable and safe closed wallet.

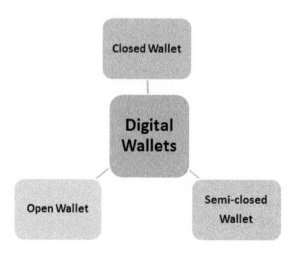

2. Semi-closed Wallet

They only listed merchants and locations to make transactions through the semi-closed wallet. The coverage area of semi-closed wallets is restricted; they can do offline and online buying through these wallets. However, merchants need to enter into contracts or agreements with the issuers for receiving payments from the mobile wallets.

3. Open Wallet

Banks or institutes incorporated with banks issue open wallets. Withdrawal of funds from banks and ATMs and funds transfer users with empty wallets can use them for all transactions allowed with a semi-closed wallet.

Examples of Digital Wallets

1. PayPal One Touch™

The PayPal One Touch™ app is addition and more latest services offered by PayPal. There is no need to the login screen and eliminate the need to enter passwords; it enables users to make payments or transfer funds faster. PayPal's mobile wallet app can also operate on a desktop, laptop, or tablet.

2. Apple Pay

The Apple Pay (as the name showed) digital app is streamlined and modernized exclusively for iPads, iPhones, and Apple watches. It facilitates users to make transactions for both online and in-store purchases., Users can unlock their phones and hold them near a compatible point of sale system for in-store transactions. The Apple Pay app enables a secure way of payments, providing ease of experience for the users.

3. Google Pay

The Google Pay app enables users to make transactions on any website or an app using a debit or credit card. Details are saved to the users' Google Account, Google Play, Chrome, YouTube, Android phones, and watches. Especially for students, the app also supports other electronic documents such as student I.D., movie tickets, gift coupons, store cards, and transportation tickets.

Chapter 2

Bitcoin

What is Bitcoin?

A decentralized digital currency that you can exchange (buy and sell) directly, without an intermediary like a central bank or single administrator, is named "Bitcoin" .It is a compound of two words, bit and coin. Satoshi Nakamoto, the creator of Bitcoin, initially described the need for "an electronic payment system instead of trust-based cryptographic proof."

Each Bitcoin transaction is accessible to everyone that has ever been made on a public ledger, hard to reverse transactions and to make it and difficult to fake. That's by design: Bitcoins' fundamental decentralized nature isn't changed by the government or any issuing institution. There's no guarantee of their value apart from the proof stored in the heart of the system.

Since it was publicly launched in 2009, Bitcoin's value has risen dramatically. While at of March 1, 2021, it once sold for under $150 per coin, and now one Bitcoin sells for almost $50,000. Because the supply is limited to 21 million coins, many expect as time goes on, its price to only keep rising, especially as institutional investors start treating it as a type of digital gold to use as a shield against market inflation and volatility.

Bitcoins are a reward of a process known as mining. Can exchange Bitcoins for other currencies, products, services, and the coins' actual value is very volatile.

Research by the University of Cambridge estimated that there were 2.9 to 5.8 million users using a cryptocurrency wallet in 2017, most of them using bitcoin. There are many reasons that users go to participate in the digital currency: beliefs such as commitment to anarchism, libertarianism, and decentralization, using as an investment, and authenticity of transactions. A desire among governments led to regulation to tax when the use of bitcoin increased, facilitated for legal help in trade, and other reasons, such as investigations for price manipulation and money laundering.

History of Bitcoin

Bitcoin is a decentralized currency that can be sent from one user to another on the peer-to-peer or multi-user bitcoin network without an intermediary. All the transactions are verified through cryptography by network nodes and recorded in a blockchain called a public distributed ledger. The cryptocurrency was first introduced in 2008 by a mysterious person or persons using the name Satoshi Nakamoto. The currency finally began use in 2009 when its performance was released as software.

For its use in illegal transactions, bitcoin often has been criticized, a large amount of electricity (and carbon footprint) used in the mining process, price volatility, and frauds from exchanges. Some economists have characterized it at different times as a speculative bubble. Bitcoin as a digital currency has also been used as an investment, even though various governing agencies have issued users alerts about bitcoin's risk.

Blockchain analysts evaluate that Satoshi Nakamoto had mined approximately one million bitcoins before disappearing in 2010 when he handed over the network alert key and control to Gavin Andresen of the code repository. Andresen became the head developer at the Bitcoin Foundation. This left opportunity for a dispute over the future development path of bitcoin, in disparity to the recognized authority of Nakamoto's efforts.

In 2011, the starting price was $0.30 per bitcoin, increasing to $5.27 in a year. On June 8, the price was rose to $31.50. then within a month, the cost of one bitcoin fell to $11.00. The following month it further dropped to $7.80, and in another month, the price was $4.77.

In 2012, the starting price of bitcoin was $5.27, increasing to $13.30 for that year. By January 9, the price decreased to $7.38, but bitcoin crashed by 49% to $3.80 for the next 16 days. On August 17, the price has then risen to $16.41, but over the next three days suddenly fell by 57% to $7.10.In September 2012, the Bitcoin Foundation was founded to develop bitcoin's growth and uptake.

In 2013, prices were started at $13.30, growing to $770 by January 1, 2014.

In March 2013, split the blockchain into two separate chains due to a bug in bitcoin's software version 0.8 with different rules. The Mt. Gox exchange during the split briefly stopped bitcoin deposits. The price decreases by 23% to $37 before take back to the past level of approximately $48 in these hours.

In 2014, the price of one bitcoin started at $770 and decreased to $314 for the year. The Wikimedia Foundation was accepting donations of bitcoin On July 30, 2014.

In 2015, prices were started at $314 and grew to $434 for the year. All around the rest of the first half of 2018, the price fluctuated from $11,480 to $5,848. Bitcoin's price was $6,343 On July 1, 2018. The price was $3,747 on January 1, 2019, fell 72% for 2018, and fell 81% since that was the all-time high price.

On March 13, 2020, the price of bitcoin fell to $4000 during a significant market selloff after trading more than $10,000 in February 2020. On March 11, 2020, a total of 281,000 bitcoins were sold out that held by holders for only thirty days. Compared to 4,131 bitcoins that had laid for a year or more dormant, indicating that day, most of the bitcoin volatility was from recent buyers. During the week of March 11, 2020, Cryptocurrency exchange Kraken was experienced that an 83% increase is shown in the number of buyer's account signups within one week of bitcoin's price fell due to buyers looking to fund in the low price.

In August 2020, MicroStrategy, as a treasury reserve asset, invested $250 million in bitcoin. In October 2020, Square, Inc. put about 1% off ($50 million) the total assets in bitcoin. PayPal announced in November 2020 that US users could buy, sell or hold bitcoin. On November 30, 2020, bitcoin reached a current all-time high value of $19,860, topping the last high value of December 2017.

Microstrategy announced on January 25, 2021, that the purchase of bitcoin continued, and it had holdings of 70,784 worth $2.38 billion as of the same date. Elon Musk placed the hold *#Bitcoin* on January 19, 2021, in Twitter profile, tweeting, "In review, it was unavoidable", which gives rise to a price of about $5000 in just an hour to $37,299. On February 8, 2021, after Tesla's announcement for a bitcoin purchase of $1.5 billion rises the bitcoin price to $44,141 as they plan to go for bitcoin as payments for vehicles.

In September 2020, the Canton of Zug, Switzerland, announced accepting tax payments in bitcoin by February 2021.

The Legislative Assembly of El Salvador In June 2021, to make Bitcoin legal tender voted legislation in El Salvador. The law further will take effect in the same year, September.

Who is Satoshi Nakamoto?

No one knows who invented bitcoin, or at least not conclusively. Satoshi Nakamoto is the name of a person or group of persons who developed the original bitcoin in 2008 and started working on the software initially released in 2009. As a part of the execution, Nakamoto also designs the first blockchain database. In this process, Satoshi Nakamoto was the first person to resolve the double-spending problem for bitcoin using an authentic peer-to-peer network. Nakamoto was very active in the progress of bitcoin until December 2010.

Although it is desirable to believe that Satoshi Nakamoto is a single, visionary genius who designs bitcoin, typically, such innovations do not happen in a vacuum. All major scientific innovations were built on formerly existing research, no matter how these discoveries original-seeming.

The Adam Back's Hashcash precursors to bitcoin: invented in 1997, and later Wei Dai's b-money, bit gold by Nick Szabo, and finally Reusable Proof of Work of Hal Finney. The bitcoin whitepaper itself mentions Hashcash and b-money, and various other works cover several fields of research. Unsurprisingly, many people behind the projects mentioned above have been assuming to have also participated in creating bitcoin. There are a few possible inspirations for bitcoin's creators deciding to keep their name or identity secret. One is privacy because bitcoin has gained popularity—a product that is becoming a broad world phenomenon—Satoshi Nakamoto would likely gather a lot of attention from media and governments.

Another reason to keep identity secret could be that bitcoin is a significant disturbance in the present banking and economic systems. If bitcoin were to gain a mass acquisition, the system could exceed nations' ruler fiat currencies. This fear about ruling money could activate governments to take legal action against bitcoin's creator.

The other primary reason is safety. In 2009, 32,489 blocks were mined; 50 bitcoin per block were the reward rate, and the total payout was 1,624,500 bitcoin in 2009. People may conclude that Satoshi and maybe a few other people through 2009 were mining and that they hold a significant part of that bitcoin stash. Someone who possesses that considerable amount of bitcoin may become a target by criminals, especially as bitcoin is more like cash and less like stocks. Authorize spending; private keys needed may be printed out and kept under a mattress. While Bitcoin's creator would take safety measures to make any blackmail-induced transfers of bitcoin traceable, remaining unidentified is an excellent way to limit exposure for Satoshi.

How does Bitcoin Work?

How exactly Bitcoin categorizes is a matter of disagreement. Is it a payment network, type of currency, an asset class, or a store of value?

What Bitcoin is easier to define. It is software. Don't consider the stock images of shiny coins embellish with a Thai baht symbol. Bitcoin is simply a digital phenomenon, a set of processes and protocols. It is the most successful after hundreds of attempts to design virtual money by using cryptography, which is the science of making and breaking codes. Hundreds of followers were inspired by bitcoin, but it remains the largest cryptocurrency by market capitalization, a difference it has held all around its decade-plus history.

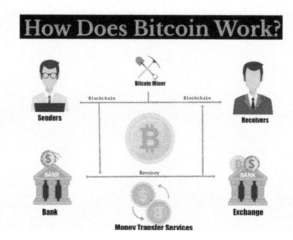

Bitcoin is a computer file stored in a computer or a smartphone in a 'digital wallet' application. People can send Bitcoins to their digital wallets, and they can transfer Bitcoins to other people. Each transaction is recorded in a blockchain which is a public list. This record of transactions makes it possible to trace the previous history of Bitcoins to stop users from spending coins that they do not own, undoing transactions, or making copies.

Buying and Selling of Bitcoin

Before Buying a Bitcoin

There are several objects that every Bitcoin investor needs. An account in cryptocurrency exchange, personal identification documents required if you are using the Know, Your Customer (KYC) platform, a method of payment, and a secure and fast connection to the Internet. It is also recommended that the buyers have their wallets outside the exchange account. Using this path, valid methods of payment include debit cards, credit cards, and bank accounts. It is also possible to buy Bitcoin from specialized ATMs and P2P exchanges. However, as of early 2020, keep in mind that Bitcoin ATMs required government-issued IDs.

For Bitcoin investors, privacy and security are significant issues. Even though bitcoin has no physical value, it is a bad idea to show off extensive holdings. Anyone who gets the private key to the public address on the blockchain can allow transactions. Private keys on the blockchain should be kept secret; because criminals may try to steal them if they learn of bitcoin's extensive holdings. Be aware that anybody can see the balance that you use on a public address.

Anyone can view a transactions history made on the blockchain. Only a user's public key is shown next to a transaction on the blockchain—making this transaction confidential but not unidentifiable. Bitcoin transactions are more transparent and detectable than cash.

FBI and the International researchers have claimed that transactions can track transactions on the blockchain to users' online accounts, including digital wallets. For example, if a person creates an account on cryptocurrency exchange Coinbase, the person must provide their identification, and when that investor purchases Bitcoin, it is tied with their name. It can still be traced if the person sends it to another wallet to the Coinbase purchase process connected with the account holder's identity. Most investors should not concern with this because Bitcoin is legal in the US and most other developed countries.

Supply and demand

Of course, supply and demand is an influencing factor in any currency, including cryptocurrencies. So this past year, the sudden popularity of Bitcoin has helped drive the price over $10,000.

There is a limited number of Bitcoin – 21 million to be exact measurements. Since there are more than seven billion people globally, if everyone could mine bitcoins easily, the currency wouldn't have much more value. But not everyone does this – so the rare do achieve a high value.

Step One: Choose an Exchange

Signing up for a cryptocurrency exchange will allow a person to hold, buy, and sell cryptocurrency. This feature may not matter for those focusing on trading Bitcoin or other cryptocurrencies. It is generally best practice to use a business to enable users to withdraw their cryptocurrency to their online wallet for safer keeping.

Cryptocurrency exchanges are of different types. Because the Bitcoin character is about individual sovereignty and decentralization, some businesses do not require users to enter personal information and allow users to remain unknown. Such exchanges operate independently and, which means they are decentralized and do not have central control. While they may use such systems for criminal activities, they are also used to give services to the world's unbanked population.

Right now, the most accepted exchanges do require KYC and are not decentralized. In the United States, these include Coinbase, Binance U.S., Gemini, and Kraken are a few. Each of these exchanges offers several features, and they have grown significantly.

When generating a cryptocurrency exchange account, an important thing to observe is to use safe internet practices. Includes using two-factor confirmation and using a unique and long password, including a variety of memorable characters, capitalized letters, lowercase letters, and numbers.

Step Two: Connect Your Exchange with Payment Option

Once the user-chosen an exchange, then it needs to accumulate personal documents. It depends on the exchange requirements; these may include social security numbers, pictures of a driver's license, and information about the source of funds and their employer. The information may need on the country they live in and the laws within the country. The process is mostly the same as opening an ordinary brokerage account.

After the exchange has confirmed the identity of the account opening person and legitimacy may now connect with the payment option. At most exchanges, users can connect a debit or credit card or can connect bank account directly. In contrast, a person can use a credit card to buy cryptocurrency. It is generally avoided for a reason is the irregularity that cryptocurrencies mainly can experience.

Although Bitcoin is legal in the United States, most banks may ask questions or even stop deposits to exchanges or crypto-related sites. It is necessary to check and make sure that the bank allows deposits in an exchange that a user chooses. Exchanges also charge per-transaction fees. This fee may be a percentage of the trading amount or a flat fee if the trading amount is low. Credit cards also incur a processing fee besides the transaction fees.

Step Three: Place an Order

In latest years, cryptocurrency exchanges have become more conventional. Once a user chooses an exchange and is connected with a payment method can now buy and sell Bitcoin and other cryptocurrencies. The functional changes at cryptocurrency exchanges are related to the shift in perception about cryptocurrencies. An industry that was considering a scam or one with questionable practices is slowly transforming into a legal one that has gained interest from all the big competitors in the financial services industry.

Once someone found an exchange and connected a payment method, he is ready to go. Now, cryptocurrency exchanges have acquired a point where all have nearly the same characteristics as their stock dealers counterparts. Today cryptocurrency exchanges offer multiple order types and methods to invest. Almost all exchanges offer both limit and market orders, and some may provide stop-loss orders.

Aside from different types of orders, exchanges also provide ways to start recurring investments that permit clients to invest their choice into average dollar costs. For example, Coinbase allows users to set frequent purchases for every day, week, or month.

Step Four: Safe Storage

For storing digital assets, Bitcoin and cryptocurrency wallets are more secure. Having crypto in the user's wallet outside of the crypto exchange makes sure that only they hold the private key to the funds. It also gives the facility store funds aside from an exchange and decreases the risk of losing their funds if the exchange gets hacked.

Some wallets have additional features than others. Some offer only Bitcoin, and some offer the facility to store various types of altcoins. Some also provide the ability to swap tokens with one another.

There are several options while choosing a bitcoin wallet. The first thing to understand about cryptocurrency wallets is that hot wallets are online wallets and cold wallets are hardware or paper wallets.

Exchanges

Understanding cryptocurrencies can be discouraging, and if a person is new to crypto trading, then finding the proper platform can be another challenge to buy and sell popular crypto-assets like Bitcoin, Litecoin, and Ethereum. Most exchanges also provide features like margin trading, staking rewards (for holding a crypto asset for a long time), crypto trading tools, and more.

The best cryptocurrency exchanges have been compiled below for buying and selling crypto assets.

Coinbase: Best Exchange for Bitcoin-oriented traders

Account Limit:

The minimum account limit is $2.

Fees:

0.50% spread for buy or sell transactions; transaction fee is from $0.99 to $2.99; up to 0.50% fee for Coinbase Pro.

Features:

Coinbase earns rewards, user-controlled storage, Coinbase Pro advanced account, stable coin staking, and institutional trading tools.

More than 50 cryptocurrencies Coinbase offers, including Bitcoin, Litecoin, Ethereum, Dogecoin, and Ripple. This exchange also offers several investment options for institutional and individual clients. Some of its available account features include iOS and Android mobile apps, staking rewards, and a Coinbase earns account option that pays in crypto assets only for watching educational videos.

Coinbase also offers to users two other options: Coinbase Prime for institutions and high-net-worth clients for individuals with a minimum of $1 million and Coinbase Pro for advance traders. Coinbase Pro users can access more up-to-date features like charting tools, secure trading bots, and real-time order books.

Binance: Best for low fees

Account Limit:

The minimum account limit is $10.

Fees:

A 0.1% spot trading fee; 0.5% instant buy or sell fee (with US debit card 4.5% fee for deposits)

Features:

Automated recurring buys, staking rewards, over-the-counter trading, crypto pairs, and institutional trading services.

In 2019 after Binance closed its services to the US traders, it then formed Binance US. The exchange is primarily for US investors, and it assists more than 50 cryptocurrencies. Like Coinbase exchange, it offers investment choices for both institutions and individuals. Some of its account benefits include staking rewards, OTC trading, recurring buys, Stablecoins (assets that are backed by US dollars), and crypto trading pairs.

Binance exchange also offers mobile access for Android and iOS devices.

Kraken: Best exchange for margin and futures traders

Account Limit:

The minimum Account limit depends on the type of cryptocurrency.

Fees:

0% - 0.26% fees applicable

Features:

Almost 60 cryptocurrencies, OTC trading, margin, and futures trading; provide account management for individuals of high-net-worth and institutional clients; educational resources, multiple trading platforms, and staking rewards.

Like other exchanges, Kraken has 50+ cryptocurrencies with many options both for retail and institutional investors. But when it comes to supporting globally, Kraken has a little more reach than Binance.US. The exchange currently in nearly 200 countries supports traders.

Kraken also offers futures trading and margin trading. With its margin accounts, users can borrow up to five times their account balance to trade crypto assets. Futures trading explained as contracts that permit users to buy or sell assets at an adjusted price on an upcoming date is available for Bitcoin, Bitcoin Cash, Litecoin, Ethereum, and Ripple.

All users can utilize Kraken's staking rewards, access to iOS and Android mobile apps, and educational resources.

CEX.IO: Best Cryptocurrency Selection

Account Limit:

The minimum account limit is $20 for a daily deposit.

Fees:

0.16% - 0.25% maker or taker transaction fees (2.99% deposit)

Features:

More than 80 cryptocurrencies, staking rewards, margin trading, institutional services, crypto-backed loans,

CEX.IO is a global crypto exchange based in London, supporting traders worldwide in more than 99% of countries, according to its website, including 48 US states. To the traders, the exchange gives access to Bitcoin and more than 80 crypto assets.

All users can easily access CEX.IO's instant buy feature (this is available only for debit and credit card purchases), staking rewards, mobile app, and crypto-backed loans. But advanced traders may prefer CEX.IO's spot trading feature (through this option lets users place different types of orders regarding the crypto market) and margin trading accounts. Businesses and institutions can use their collective and payment management services.

Its taker fees range from 0.1-0.25%, and maker fees span from 0-.016%. Users can also access CEX.IO on Android or iOS devices.

Gemini: Best Crypto Exchange for Bitcoin and Ethereum traders

Account Limit:

There is no minimum account limit.

Fees:

$0.99-$2.99 fee for mobile and web transactions between $10 to $200 (1.49% fee applicable for transactions over $200); 3.49% debit card transfers, and 0.50% convenience fee.

Features:

Trading options for institutions, beginners, and experts; Gemini Wallet, Gemini Earn, and in Gemini Custody, there is $200 million insurance.

Gemini offers a wide variety of crypto trading services for institutions and individuals. Users can take advantage of several platforms, including the Gemini Active Trader platform, Gemini web exchange, Gemini Fund Solutions, Gemini iOS, Android mobile apps, and institutional trading tools.

But the exchange also gives a few other outstanding features: Gemini Earn, Gemini Wallet, Gemini Clearing (trading services for off-exchange crypto trades between the parties), Gemini Pay, Gemini Custody, and Gemini Dollar (digital asset support by US dollars). Though Gemini exchange isn't only a personal wallet service, its two custody and storage options — Gemini Custody and Gemini Wallet— give the choice of institutional offline storage or online storage for user's crypto assets. In cold storage insurance coverage, Gemini custody also offers $200 million.

Gemini Earn gives the option to receive up to 7.4% interest on the crypto balance, while Gemini Pay gives the chance to use assets for purchases at more than 30,000 retail provisions across the US.

Bittrex: Best Exchange for account security

Account Limit:

The maximum account limit is $3.

Fees:

0-0.35% maker or taker fees.

Features:

Instant buy or sell, mobile access, highly secure cold storage.

Bittrex is difficult to beat when the point comes to account security. In addition to two-factor authentication, to ensure funds are kept secure, the exchange uses a multi-stage wallet strategy, cold storage (offline storage). As compared to other exchanges, Bittrex's transaction fees are also lower.

Like CEX.IO, the exchange utilizes a maker or taker fee schedule based on the trader's 30-day trading capacity (the number of total crypto assets exchanged over the past 30 days). But unlike other investment apps, Bittrex charges nothing for deposits (USD withdrawals and deposits have no fees either). However, Blockchain or crypto withdrawals have small network fees. Users can access Bittrex on Android or iOS phones

Other exchanges to be considered

Bitstamp:

Bitstamp is a Luxembourg-based exchange offering about 20 cryptocurrencies, with options for institutional traders and advanced traders. US users through its subsidiary, Bitstamp USA. Can trade crypto assets. While the lowest fees start at 0.5%, traders will need at least $50 to trade.

Abra:

Abra is a mobile-based crypto exchange offering more than 100 cryptocurrencies, including bitcoin, dogecoin, ethereum, and others. The exchange also provides safe storage services, loans (with 0% interest rates), interest account options, and more. While its geographic range extends to the US and 150 other countries, the app's fees for credit card transactions are on the higher side.

SoFi:

SoFi than a cryptocurrency exchange, is more of an online brokerage, but it currently offers only three crypto-assets: Bitcoin, Litecoin, and Ethereum. The exchange app also fee a 1.25% markup on all the crypto transactions, meaning traders will receive an extra 1.25% on the final price of the share(s). The downside is that SoFi's crypto assets options are limited, and users bear higher fees than other exchanges.

eToro:

The eToro crypto exchange provides highly secure and easily navigable communication that gives access to approximately 16 crypto assets. The exchange also assists traders in 140 countries, but traders to deposit funds will need at least $50 and trade $25. eToro currently doesn't support traders in New York, New Hampshire, Delaware, Nevada, Minnesota, American Samoa, Puerto Rico, Hawaii, Guam, Tennessee, and the US Virgin Islands.

Webull:

This online brokerage exchange only requires $1 to start trading crypto assets but is limited to its investment selection. Webull may not be the best option if someone wants to trade crypto other than Bitcoin, Bitcoin Cash, Dogecoin, Litecoin, Ethereum, Stellar, or Zcash.

Robinhood:

This commission-free brokerage structure has quite attracted those who choose low-cost investments, but like Webull and SoFi, Robinhood's crypto selection is somehow on the shorter side. This app only offers Bitcoin, Bitcoin SV, Bitcoin Cash, Dogecoin, Litecoin, Ethereum, and Ethereum Classic.

Bitcoin Mining

Evolution of Mining

In the early 2000s, at the beginning stages of Bitcoin, people interested in Bitcoin mining were allowed to do so by using their personal computers. As Bitcoin's popularity increased, so did the difficulty of mining.

Assist the growing level of difficulty, additional computer processing power was required. In a short time, miners used gaming computers to mine Bitcoin. As the process repeated, the mining difficulty and the required amount of computing power increased.

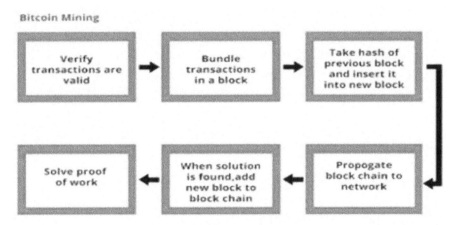

Ultimately, computers and chips were designed for mining Bitcoin. Today, it requires systematic and efficient hardware – those with energy efficiency and strong computing abilities. Solving the Bitcoin algorithm adds to the blockchain, and receiving Bitcoin requires a massive amount of electricity. Making Bitcoin mining process profitable and sustainable, the key is keeping electricity costs low.

How Does Bitcoin Mining Work?

Bitcoin mining is the process of add up new transactions to the blockchain. It's a very tough job. People who decided to mine Bitcoin should use a process called proof of work; in this position, computers in a competition solve mathematical puzzles to verify transactions.

There was a possibility for the average person that mine Bitcoin in the earliest days, but that's not possible for a long time. The Bitcoin codes are written for solving its puzzles more challenging over time, requiring complex computing resources. Now, Bitcoin mining is possible through powerful computers and access to huge amounts of low-price electricity to be successful.

Bitcoin mining pays less than it used, making it even harder to recover the rising computative and electrical costs.

Basics of Bitcoin Mining

There are three basic methods to acquire Bitcoin:

1. Purchase Bitcoin on an exchange
2. Receive goods and services in exchange
3. Mine a new Bitcoin

How Does Cryptocurrency Mining Work?

Cryptocurrency mining work for two vital purposes:

1. Mining releases the new cryptocurrency coins in the network
2. Mining verifies all transactions made on the network

Cryptocurrency mining involves solving massive computational equations that involve matching a 64-digit hexadecimal hash. Matching and comparing hashes at the extra high rate required by cryptocurrency networks that's why mining requires expensive hardware.

The rates are measured in mega hash per second (MH/s), tetra hash per second (TH/s), Giga hash per second (GH/s), and very recently, exa hash per second (EH/s).

The Bitcoin network goal is to release a new block after every ten minutes. But as increases the number of miners on the network, it becomes more likely for a miner to match the correct hash quickly. That's where difficulty in mining comes into play.

As the total hash rate increases, so does the level of the mining process become difficult—the network difficulty changes after every 2016 block. If the discovery time is less than 10 minutes and the hash rate is high, then the difficulty level increases. But if the block discovery process takes more than 10 minutes, then the difficulty level decreases. As soon as a miner matches a hash and verifies 1 MB of transactions, that miner becomes eligible for the reward. The block reward is the final Bitcoin network payout for verifying the transactions.

Pros and Cons of Bitcoin Mining

Here, we look at some of the potential advantages and disadvantages of cryptocurrencies.

Advantages

1. Potential of high returns

Over the last five years, the price of bitcoin has compounded in USD at an annualized growth rate of 131.5%.

2. Potential diversification

Some have quoted cryptocurrencies as another instrument to gold in a portfolio context. In the five years to the end of 2020, a portfolio including 10% invested in bitcoin would have generated annual returns of 26.8%.

3. Limited supply

There is a maximum of 21 million coins that can be mined or created. The rate of production of bitcoins slows over time through a process known as halving. In 2009, each block was worth 50 bitcoins, but now the value is 6.25 bitcoins per block.

4. Protection from low-value currencies and threat of rising inflation

Some people suggest cryptocurrencies offer alternatives that cannot be debated in the national currencies and increase inflation.

5. Growing acceptance and usage of Bitcoin

It is essential to notice that there has been a tremendous increase over the past few years in the number of bitcoin electronic wallets created. There are a multiplying number of institutional investors looking to invest in cryptocurrencies.

Disadvantages

1. High uncertainty and potential for large losses

The annualized uncertainty in the price of bitcoin in US dollars is changed about 90% per month as measured over the five years. Investment in bitcoin or other crypto assets, the timing will have a significant impact on the returns achieved.

2. Correlations

People could argue that Bitcoin has a lousy record of giving diversification benefits when they are needed. Historically, bitcoin's correlation to other traditional assets has been very low. But lately, its correlation has been rising.

3. Endless potential supply

The number of bitcoins created will finally be limited to 21 million. Many other cryptocurrencies have a limited supply to their protocols. Currently, many new cryptocurrencies are being launched. Therefore, the supply of cryptocurrency is potentially limitless.

4. Poor store of value and limited acceptance

While bitcoin and some cryptocurrencies are now accepted across an extended number of payment platforms, the number of places remains very limited. One can exchange cryptocurrencies for tangible goods or services. For this reason, the volatility in cryptocurrencies makes them a poor store of value; the fact is when converted into an individual's currency, the value of crypto will change wildly even within a day.

5. Unregulated and unbacked

Cryptocurrencies are a formation of the private sector with no official regulation. Mean that cryptocurrencies are extensively open to being misused by criminals in a way to scam unwary investors. A 2019 academic study research that 25% of users of bitcoin are involved in illegal activities and that 46% of transactions are linked with illegal activity.

Bitcoin Wallets

What is a Bitcoin wallet?

Bitcoin wallet is a software application in which users store their Bitcoins. Bitcoin does not exist in any physical form or shape. It can't technically be stored in Bitcoin except for coin wallets anywhere. This type of software is simple to use and authentic while also being fast and secure.

First, users need to decide the amount of Bitcoin they want to buy. After that, they need to enter an amount that they want to deposit to their bitcoin address. Using ACH, credit card, Wire will then transferred the amount to the Bitcoin wallet.

1) Coinbase

Coinbase is a cryptocurrency wallet used for transferring, purchasing, selling, and storing digital currency. In offline storage, it securely stores a large range of digital assets. This crypto wallet facilitates more than 100 countries.

Features:

Can buy and sell digital currencies and keep them tracking in one place.

It provides an app for Android and iOS devices.

Users can schedule their currency trading on a daily, weekly, or monthly basis.

For safety purposes, it stores funds in a wallet.

Coinbase is one of the largest crypto exchanges.

For signing up, get $5 in free Bitcoin.

2) Binance

One of the best places to create a bitcoin wallet is Binance that offers users a platform for trading about 150 digital currencies. It provides an API that helps traders to integrate their current trading applications.

Features:

This application provides a wide range of tools for online trading.

Binance is one of the safest bitcoin wallets that provides its users 24/7 support.

This app is compatible with Android, iOS, Web, and PC clients.

Binance for trading provides advanced and basic exchange interfaces.

Over 1,400,000 transactions per second it does 1.2 billion average daily trading volume.

3) Kraken

Kraken is a tough competitor of Coinbase. It also provides financial stability by maintaining whole reserves, the highest legal compliance standards, and relationships.

Features:

A very comprehensive security approach.

Allows individuals to buy and sell crypto assets in a single click.

Through live chat, users can reach out to their support team.

Kraken automatically checks errors for all addresses.

4) Gemini

Gemini is an entirely regulated exchange. It helps clients authorize cryptocurrencies worldwide—the exchange trades in cryptos, including Bitcoin, Bitcoin Cash, Ethereum, Litecoin, etc.

Features:

It is a very simple, secure, and elegant way to set up Bitcoin and crypto portfolios.

For volume, traders offer up to 0% discounts.

Offer standard security measures.

Regulation identical to trust for most investors.

5) Trezor

The Trezor wallet helps users to store their bitcoins. Users can easily plug into their computer or smartphone. It helps to generate randomly a pin code that keeps the devices safe and secure.

Features:

Offline storage is ultra-secure.

Trezor facilitates more than 1,000 currencies.

An easy-to-use touchscreen.

Extremely simple wallet to use.

It allows users to expose their private keys.

Supported platforms: Linux, Windows, or Mac OS X.

6) CEX.IO

Cex.io is a platform that helps users to buy and sell Bitcoins. It offers users to deposit their funds using MasterCard, PayPal Debit MasterCard, or Visa card. This online program uses frequency and scalping trading strategies to secure both assets and data.

Features:

Users can trade USD, XRP (Ripple), and Ethereum (an open-source distributed calculating platform) for Bitcoins.

Using full data encryption, it protects against DDOS(Distributed Denial-of-Service) attacks.

Without creating a new account, users can trade with more than 10x leverage.

CEX.IO supports platforms including mobile devices and websites.

In more than 35 states of the USA, CEX.IO gives service.

This application also offers downloadable reports that are showing real-time transaction and balance history.

7) Changelly

Changelly is one of the best crypto exchanges that enable users to exchange crypto assets fast and buy them with a bank card. It also provides a facility to trade BTC (Bitcoin), LTC(Litecoin), ETH, and XRP.

Features:

Users can easily check the best rates that are currently available in the market.

For exchanging transactions, traders don't require any verification.

Changelly supports more than 150 cryptocurrencies.

Take benefit of the features; the Changelly application offers API.

8) Nash

Without any hassle, Nash is one of the best places to buy crypto. It provides fast trading across Bitcoin, Ethereum, NEO blockchains, and more. This application enables users quickly to set their transaction limit.

Features:

It is available in more languages like English, Italian, French, and Portuguese.

It secures user's wallets using encryption.

Nash supports a quick payment method.

Users can easily receive their cryptocurrency amount in wallets.

Its supported platforms are iOS and Android devices.

Chapter 3

Altcoin

What is Altcoin?

Altcoins are cryptocurrencies that don't include Bitcoin. The word 'Altcoin' combines two words, where alt means 'alternative' and the word coin means 'cryptocurrency'. Together, they include a cryptocurrency category, which is an alternative to Bitcoin, a digital currency. They share characteristics similar to Bitcoin but are different in other ways. For example, some altcoins use a different mechanism to produce blocks or verify transactions. Or, they differentiate themselves from Bitcoin by offering new or additional abilities, such as low-price volatility or intelligent contracts.

There are almost 9,000 cryptocurrencies as of March 2021. According to CoinMarketCap, altcoins consider for over 40% of the total crypto market in March 2021. The reason is they are derived from Bitcoin; Altcoin price changes tend to copy Bitcoin's trajectory. Most altcoins that have been released are built on the same blockchain technology that spread bitcoin. This technology is already assisting more efficient and secure ways of business transactions and transferring assets.

In the last few years, because of the expansion of cryptocurrency and the wave of programmers and developers looking to turn into cash on the rise of alternative payment systems, the altcoin market is full of choices.

How Do Altcoins Work?

Generally speaking, altcoins work more like the original Bitcoin. Using a private key, users can send a payment from their digital wallet to another user's wallet. In a cryptocurrency such as Altcoins, there is a blockchain, or a recording ledger, where the transactions are publicly and permanently recorded, so exchanges can not be denied or altered after the fact.

This blockchain is secured through mathematics proofs which should confirm transactions in blocks.

Different kinds of Altcoins.

Depending on their features and consensus mechanisms, altcoins come in different categories. Below is a summary of some more essential Altcoins:

Mining-Based

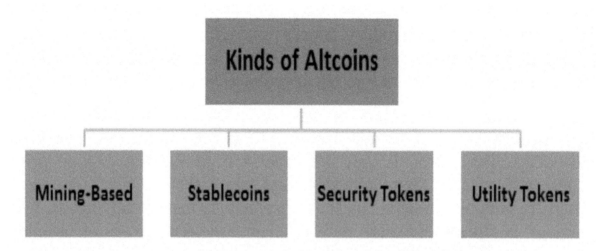

Mining-based altcoins, as their name indicates, are mined into existence. Most mining-based altcoins use a method called Proof-of-Work (PoW), in which systems produce new coins by solving complex problems to create blocks. Examples of mining-based altcoins include Litecoin, Zcash, and Monero. Top of the altcoins fell into the mining-based category in early 2020. Such coins are not generated by an algorithm but are issued before they are listed in crypto markets. Ripple's XRP is an example of a pre-mined coin.

Stablecoins

Cryptocurrency use and trading have been noticeable by volatility since launch. Stablecoins aim to decrease this overall volatility by fixing their value to a basket of goods, such as precious metals, fiat currencies, or other cryptocurrencies. The basket acts as a reserve to reclaim holders if the cryptocurrency faces problems fails. Price variations for stablecoins are not directly meant to increase a narrow range.

Facebook's Diem, a social media behemoth, is the most famous example of a stable coin. Diem is a dollar-backed coin. Other examples of stablecoins are MakerDAO and USDC.

Security Tokens

Security tokens are as similar as securities traded in stock markets. Security tokens resemble traditional stocks, and they frequently promise equity, a dividend pay-out to holders, or ownership form. The possibility of price appreciation for these tokens is an essential draw for investors to invest money into them. Besides, they have a digital source. Security tokens are generally provided to investors through the initial coin offerings or ICOs.

Utility Tokens

Utility tokens are used to give services within a network. For example, they possibly used to redeem rewards or purchase services. Unlike security tokens, utility tokens are not part of an ownership stake or pay-out dividends. An example of a utility token is Filecoin, used to purchase storage space in a network.

Are Altcoin Good Investment?

The market of altcoins is just beginning. In the last decade, the number of altcoins listed in crypto markets has quickly multiplied and attracted a crowd of retail investors, excitedly betting on their price changes to amass short-term profits. But these investors do not have the necessary capital to generate adequate market liquidity.

In the case of Ethereum's ether, consider, which reached the highest value of $1299.95 on Jan 12, 2018. Not more than a month later, it was decreased to $597.36, and at the end of the year, ether's price had further crashed to $89.52. The record prices of Altcoin reached above $2,000 two years later.

But the problem is, the cryptocurrency markets are not mature yet. Despite several attempts, there are no defined investment standards or metrics to estimate cryptocurrencies. Most parts of the altcoin market were driven by speculation. Majority of the cases of dead cryptocurrencies, those which failed to gain adequate traction or simply disappear after gathering investors' money, exist.

Therefore, for investors, the altcoin market is ready to take on the massive risk of operating in a deregulated and known market prone to volatility. They should also be able to control stress arise from wild price swings. Cryptocurrency markets offer significant returns for these investors.

Advantages

Altcoins are "greater versions" of Bitcoin because the purpose is to plug the shortcomings of cryptocurrency.

Like stablecoins, altcoins can potentially accomplish Bitcoin's original promise of a means for daily transactions.

Certain altcoins, such as Ripple's XRP and Ethereum's ether, have already obtained traction among recognized institutions, which results in high valuations.

Investors can choose a wide range of altcoins that carry out different functions in the cryptocurrency economy

Disadvantages

As compared to Bitcoin, altcoins have a comparatively smaller investment market. Bitcoin has a 60% share of the cryptocurrency market as of April 2021.

The regulation and explained criteria for investment mean that some investors and low liquidity characterize the altcoin market. As a result, as compared to Bitcoin, their prices are more volatile.

To distinguish between different and relevant altcoins, it is not always easy, use cases making investment decisions more difficult and confusing.

Various "dead" altcoins result in sinking investor dollars.

Top 10 Altcoins for 2021

There are thousands of different cryptocurrencies like Bitcoin and Ethereum to Dogecoin and Tether; this can make it overwhelming when a person first entered the crypto world. Following cryptocurrencies are the top 10 based on the market capitalization or the total value of all coins currently in circulation.

1) Bitcoin (BTC)

Market cap: Over $641 billion

Bitcoin (BTC) is the first original cryptocurrency created in 2009 by an unknown person, the pseudonym Satoshi Nakamoto. As with many cryptocurrencies, BTC operated on a blockchain or a ledger register transactions distributed over a network of thousands of computers.

Bitcoin has become a household name its price has skyrocketed. Five years ago, someone could buy a Bitcoin for about $500.But now, a single Bitcoin's price is over $33,000.

2) Ethereum (ETH)

Market cap: Over $307 billion

Both a blockchain platform and a cryptocurrency, Ethereum is a favorite for program developers because of its possible applications, like the smart contracts that automatically carry out when conditions are met and also non-fungible tokens (NFTs).

Ethereum has also experienced enormous growth. In just five years, its price proceeds from about $11 to over $2,500.

3) Tether (USDT)

Market cap: Over $62 billion

Unlike other forms of cryptocurrency, Tether (USDT) is a stablecoin, which means it's backed by fiat currencies more like the Euro and the U.S. dollars and supposedly keeps the value equal to one of those denominations. This means that Tether's value is expected to be more stable than other cryptocurrencies and is favored by investors who are very cautious of the excessive volatility of other coins.

4) Binance Coin (BNB)

Market cap: Over $56 billion

The Binance Coin is a form of cryptocurrency that a person can use to pay fees and trade on Binance, one of the world's largest crypto exchanges.

Since this coin launch in 2017 has spread past, ultimately facilitating trades on its Binance exchange platform. Now, it is used for payment processing, trading, or even booking travel arrangements. It can also be exchanged or traded for other cryptocurrencies, such as Bitcoin or Ethereum.

Its price was just $0.10 in 2017; by June 2021, it had increased over $350.

5) Cardano (ADA)

Market cap: Over $51 billion

Later to the crypto scene, Cardano is noticeable for its early acceptance of proof-of-stake validation. This method accelerates transaction time and reduces energy usage and environmental effect by removing the competitive, problem-solving factor of transaction verification present in platforms like Bitcoin. To enable decentralized applications and smart contracts, Cardano also works as Ethereum, which is powered by its native coin ADA.

As compared to other major crypto coins, Cardano's ADA token has had relatively slow growth. ADA's price was $0.02; in 2017, its price was $1.50, as of June 2021.

6) Dogecoin (DOGE)

Market cap: Over $44 billion

Thanks to billionaires like Elon Musk and celebrities, Dogecoin has been a very hot topic. In 2013 famously started as a joke, Dogecoin quickly became a well-known cryptocurrency option, thanks to creating memes and a dedicated community. Unlike Bitcoin and many other cryptos, there is no limit on the Dogecoin numbers that can create, which leaves the currency sensitive to devaluation as supply increases.In 2017 price of one Dogecoin was $0.0002. By June 2021, its price had risen to $0.32.

7) Ripple (XRP)

Market cap: Over $40 billion

XRP, created by some similar founders as Ripple, a payment processing and digital technology company, can facilitate exchanges of various currency types includes fiat currencies and other famous cryptocurrencies.

The price of XRP at the beginning of 2017 was $0.006. As of June 2021, its price was at $0.92.

8) USD Coin (USDC)

Market cap: Over $23 billion

USD Coin (USDC) is a stablecoin like Tether, and, andU.S. dollars back, the goal is 1 USD to 1 USDC ratio. Ethereum also powers USDC, and users can use USD Coin to settle global transactions

9) Polkadot (DOT)

Market cap: Over $21 billion

Cryptocurrencies may use several blockchains; Polkadot goals to merge them by creating a network that connects the different blockchains to work together. This combination may facilitate how cryptocurrencies are managed and have encouraged impressive growth as Polkadot's launch in 2020. Its price grew from $2.93 to $20.95 between September 2020 to June 2021.

10) Uniswap (UNI)

Market cap: Over $13 billion

Uniswap (UNI) is an Ethereum-based token powered by Uniswap, a decentralized cryptocurrency exchange that for trading uses an automated liquidity model. This means that there is no central facilitator, as a broker-dealer or bank. Rather, it is powered by smart contracts and by the pooled user resources. Uniswap's platform is open source, so anyone to creates their exchanges can use the code.

Difference between Bitcoin and Altcoins

Safety Tips Investing in Altcoin

The process of investing in cryptocurrency has been made very simpler over the last few months. Below are some important factors that investors must think about before buying a cryptocurrency:

Location

To find out where and how to buy cryptocurrency is important for investors to check their country's regulations.

Payment Method

The most familiar and accepted payment methods include bank transfer, credit card, or even cash for buying cryptocurrency. Different exchanges accept different payment methods, so buyers need to choose an exchange that accepts the payment method they want to use.

Type of Cryptocurrency

All cryptocurrencies are not available to purchase on every exchange. The buyer will have to find first an exchange that sells the cryptocurrency that he wants to buy.

Cost of Fees

Each exchange has different fees. Make sure how much will be fees cost before setting up an account.

How Much You Can Afford

As with any investment, a buyer should never invest more than they can afford. It is also recommended that before making any investment, investors are first speaking to a financial adviser.

Risky Transaction

Before signing up for an exchange, study the cryptocurrency market and don't invest in risky transactions, at least when to start with.

Avoid Ponzi Schemes

Before investing, carefully examine altcoins to avoid Ponzi schemes

Use of Offline Wallet

Investors should keep the bulk of cryptocurrency in an offline (cold) wallet and their passwords in a safe place.

Free Coin Promises

Don't attract to promises of free coins, even or especially from celebrities: Their accounts possibly have been hacked, or even if they haven't, it is almost indeed a deception.

Protected Internet Connection

Protect internet connection, and install antivirus software on all devices which a user uses for crypto trading.

Where to obtain Altcoin?

Take a look at the list of the six best crypto exchanges for altcoins.

Best for Active Investors: eToro

eToro is a great choice if someone wants to actively involve in cryptocurrencies. eToro has a distinctive social media platform on its exchange and offers users to communicate their trading ideas with each other.

Learn about cryptocurrency; eToro is an excellent place for beginners as long as it has this built-in platform. Many beginners observe eToro as a simple interface and easy to learn. Also, eToro has a distinctive feature called CopyTrader, where users can allot a portion of their funds to mimic famous trader's portfolios.

Best for Mobile Users: Gemini

Gemini is a cryptocurrency exchange, provides a great choice for mobile users. It offers a smooth mobile app for Android and iOS to manage their crypto on the go. Gemini, currently on its exchange, offers bitcoin and also 25 different altcoins.

Users on Gemini can also get an insured wallet that protects them from online security breaches. Users can point to several cryptocurrency hacks throughout the years, so it is good to have an additional layer of security like insurance. If you purchase a hardware wallet, then investors don't have insurance.

Best for Beginners: Coinbase

Suppose a beginner who wants to invest in cryptocurrencies should first take a look at Coinbase. Coinbase provides about 40 different altcoins to choose a cryptocurrency, and it offers a significantly unique feature where users can automatically convert any altcoin into another altcoin through its exchange. Coinbase can do this only because it is a crypto brokerage, not a crypto exchange. The two altcoins are not traded for each other. Coinbase just credits the user's account with the correct tokens.

For iOS and Android, Coinbase offers a crypto website and a mobile app. To fund their account, users can connect to your bank through credit card or wire. While on the other hand, traders of crypto send cryptocurrency to their Coinbase wallet to fund accounts.

Best for DeFi Exchanges: Crypto.com

Crypto.com is a cryptocurrency platform that allows users to store, exchange, and transfer more than 90 cryptocurrencies. It also offers Crypto.com's Visa Card, so users can spend their crypto anywhere while Visa Card is generally accepted and earn up to 8% back.

Crypto.com can get investors to verified in less than 5 minutes, and it has no fees to open an account. Crypto.com offers 24/7 customer support.

Furthermore, the Visa card, Crypto.com products include its app, Crypto Earn, Crypto Pay, the Crypto.com Exchange, and DeFi Wallet and Crypto Credit. Crypto.com wants to speed up the world's transformation to cryptocurrency, and its broad range of products can help people start their processes.

Best for Ethereum: Argent

Argent is not an exchange; it is an Ethereum wallet. Traders can exchange altcoins directly on their mobile app; that's why it is included in this list. As Argent is an Ethereum wallet, so users can hold any Ethereum-based token. Examples of some tokens on Ethereum's Blockchain include Binance Coin, Uniswap, ChainLink, and WBTC.

Argent also allows users to interact with various decentralized financed (DeFi) applications create on Ethereum. It is probably Argent's best feature because it authorizes users to earn interest on their cryptocurrency investments. Interest rates can extend over as high as 50% annual returns on these platforms, depending on the crypto a person holds in his account.

Argent supports more tokens than exchanges because it supports only Ethereum-based tokens so that investors will tap into less variety. Most investors care about the quality of altcoins on an exchange compared to the number of altcoins offered on an exchange.

Best for Altcoin Variety: Binance

A leading cryptocurrency exchange Binance, with many built-in features, offers users the option to trade against bitcoin, USDT trading pairs, or U.S.

dollars. (USDT is a stablecoin fixed with the U.S. dollar and with the U.S. dollar has a 1:1 ratio.) Binance also has its token, Binance coin (BNB), that users can use to pay transaction fees.

Depending on location, Binance also offers financial derivatives. It offers margin trading in some regions and allows users to leverage their crypto positions. Of the exchanges discussed above, Binance has a wide variety of altcoins. Binance supports over 500 trading pairs and 184 different cryptocurrencies.

Chapter 4

Blockchain Technology

What is Blockchain Technology?

Imagine a world where we can spend money without a bank directly to someone within seconds instead of days, and we don't pay excessive bank fees. Or we can store cash in an online wallet that is not tied to a bank, meaning we are our bank and have complete control over our money. We don't need a bank's permission to move or access it and never have to worry because of a third party or a government's economic strategy manipulating it.

It is not a world of the future; it is a world where an eager but expanded number of early adopters live right now. And these are a few of the blockchain technology use cases that are changing the way we trust and exchange value. Blockchain technology is still an intimidating or even mysterious topic. Some even remain doubtful that they will use this technology in the future.

Blockchain definitely can be complicated, but its basic concept is quite simple. A blockchain is technically a type of database. To be able to understand blockchain, first to understand what a database is.

A database is defined as a collection of information that is electronically stored on a computer system. Data or information in databases is generally structured in table format to allow it easier searching and screening for specific details. What is the difference between using a spreadsheet instead of a database to store information?

Spreadsheets are designed to store and access limited information for one person or a small group of people. On the other hand, a database is intended for significantly larger amounts of information that can be filtered, accessed, and operated quickly and easily by the number of users at once.

Large databases reach this by housing data on servers that are made up of powerful computers. Sometimes, these servers can build by using hundreds or thousands of computers to have the storage capacity and computational power necessary for several users to access the database simultaneously. While a database or spreadsheet may be accessible to some users, it is sometimes owned by a business and managed by an individual appointed with command over how it works and manages data.

Working Mechanism of Blockchain.

Over the last few years, many businesses around the world incorporating Blockchain technology. But the question is, how exactly does blockchain technology work? Is this a simple addition or a significant change? The progress of blockchain is still young and has the energy to be revolutionary in the future; so, let's start explaining this technology.

Blockchain is a combination of the following three leading technologies:

1. Cryptographic keys
2. A peer-to-peer network consisting of a shared ledger
3. A means of calculating to store the records and transactions of the network

Cryptography keys consist of Private keys and Public keys. These keys help in executing successful transactions between two parties. Both individuals have these two keys, which they use to generate a secure digital identity reference. The secured identity is an essential feature of Blockchain technology. This identity is referred to as a 'digital signature' in the cryptocurrency world used to control and authorize transactions.

The digital signature is integrated with the peer-to-peer network, where many individuals act as authorities use a digital signature to reach consent on transactions, among other issues. When they agree to a deal, it is certified through a mathematical verification, which generates a successful secured transaction between two network-connected parties. So to summarize it, Blockchain users use cryptography keys to carry out different types of digital communications over the peer-to-peer network.

Transaction Process

One of blockchain technology's primary features is the way it confirms and authorizes transactions. For example, if two individuals want to perform a transaction with private and public keys, the first person would attach the transaction information to the public key of the second person. This information is gathered at one place into a block. This block contains a timestamp, a digital signature, and other important and relevant information. Identities of individuals involved in the transaction don't include in the block. This block is then transmitted all across the network's nodes. Whenever the right user or individual uses his private key and matches it with the block, the transaction gets completed successfully.

When conducting financial transactions, the blockchain can also record transactional details of vehicles, properties, etc. Here is a use case to illustrate how blockchain works:

Hash Encryptions

Blockchain uses hash encryption to secure the information depending mainly on the SHA256 algorithm. The sender's address (public key), the address of the receiver, his/her private key, and the transaction details are transmitted via the SHA256 algorithm. The hash encryption (called encrypted information) is transmitted worldwide and, after verification, added to the blockchain. The SHA256 algorithm makes it impossible to hack the hash encryption, simplifying the sender and receiver's authentication.

Proof of Work

In a Blockchain, each and all block consists of 4 main headers.

Previous Hash

This hash address containing the address of the previous block.

Transaction Details

Details of all transactions that need to occur.

Nonce

An arbitrary number specified in cryptography to differentiate the hash address of the block.

Hash Address of the Block:

All of the above are transmitted through a hashing algorithm. This process gives an output containing a 256-bit length value of 64 characters called the distinctive 'hash address.' As a result, it is referred to as the hash of the block.

Various people worldwide try to find the right hash value to reach a predetermined condition using computational algorithms. The transaction is completed when the predetermined condition is met. Blockchain miners try to solve a mathematical puzzle, which is a proof of work problem. Whoever first solves it gets a reward.

Mining

In Blockchain technology, adding transactional details in the present public/digital ledger is called 'mining.' However, the term is connected with Bitcoin. It is used to mention other Blockchain technologies as well. Mining requires generating the hash of a block transaction, which is very difficult to counterfeit, therefore ensuring the safety of the blockchain without needing a central system.

What are the Implications of Blockchain Technology?

Blockchain technology has a significant impact on society, including:

Bitcoin, blockchain's main application and the basic reason developed the technology in the first place, has helped many people through financial services like digital wallets. It allowed micropayments and provided microloans to people in fewer than ideal economic circumstances, introducing new life in the world economy.

The next impact is the concept of TRUST, especially within the field of international transactions. In previous days, hired lawyers crossed over the trust gap between two parties, but this consumed extra time and money. The introduction of cryptocurrency has entirely changed the trust equation. Various organizations are located in areas where resources are inadequate, and corruption is common. In such cases, blockchain provides a significant advantage to these people and organizations, allowing them to break out the tricks of untrustworthy third-party intermediaries.

In politics, blockchain is considered by an organization named Follow My Vote, which is trying to take action against election fraud at the ballot box.

The appearance of the Internet of Things (IoT) has released an excess of smart machines that move data over the internet without human interaction. In addition, technology is also used for public services such as transportation, traffic management, and rubbish collection. So, in the world of IoT, people can make smart contracts and authorize smart objects to perform the listed tasks, which in turn invalidate the need for human involvement, thus improving the transparency of the entire system.

Blockchain technology also creates a decentralized peer-to-peer network for apps like Uber and Airbnb or organizations. Through Blockchain technology, people restrict to pay for things like parking, toll fees, etc.

Blockchain technology is used as a secure place for the healthcare industry; the purpose is to store sensitive patients data. Health-related organizations like hospitals can produce a centralized database with blockchain technology and share the information with only authorized people.

Blockchain technology can be approached by two parties who want to conduct a private transaction in the private consumer sphere. Fortunately, since Blockchain technology is in work, a distributed ledger shared ledger or any other network, the parties can quickly obtain answers to the exchange relation queries. Also, information or transactions can be tracked from the departure point to the destination point by all supply chain users.

In a traditional database, users have to trust a system administrator not to change the data. But, there is no possibility of altering the data or changing the data; the data stored inside the blockchain is permanent; one cannot undo or delete it.

All of the above examples are verify that Blockchain technology is here to remain to continue and will be an important source in the future.

Types of Blockchains

Following are four types of Blockchain:

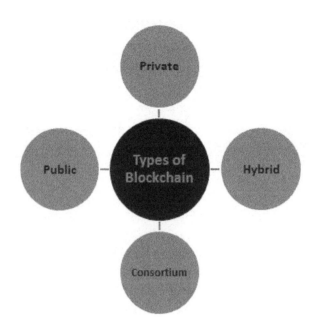

1. Public Blockchains

Public blockchains refer to decentralized networks of computers reachable to anyone wanting to request or validate a transaction (check for accuracy). Miners who verify transactions consecutively receive rewards.

Public blockchains use proof-of-stake or proof-of-work consensus mechanisms. Two common examples of public blockchains are the Bitcoin and Ethereum (ETH) blockchains.

2. Private Blockchains

Private blockchains have access restrictions, and they are not open. They are typically controlled by one entity, meaning that they are centralized. People who want to join a private blockchain require permission from the system administrator. For example, Hyperledger is a private and permissioned blockchain.

3. Hybrid Blockchains or Consortiums

Consortiums or Hybrid Blockchains combine private and public blockchains and contain centralized and decentralized features—for example, Dragonchain, Energy Web Foundation, and R3.

4. Sidechains

A blockchain running parallel to the main chain is named a sidechain. Liquid Network is an example of a sidechain. It allows users to move crypto assets between two different blockchains and improves efficiency and scalability.

Real-life use of Blockchains

First, considering the hype and popularity gained by blockchain technology in the past years, it wouldn't be amazing to say that blockchain technology is a game-changer and is considered the next big thing following the invention of the internet. In simple words, it holds a record of each transaction that everyone can easily access, eliminating the need for a central authority.

Following are some real-world applications of Blockchain technology covering various industries, which exhibit substance beyond the hype.

1. Supply chain management

Blockchains technology increases the overall efficiency of supply chains. It provides accurate location identification of items on the supply chain. So that it removes the need for paper-based trials, it helps prevent losses and monitor the quality of the products while in production.

2. Digital IDs

With an estimated 1 billion people worldwide not having an identity, Microsoft is working on generating IDs to empower refugees and impoverished people. It would work when linking them with the formal financial sector. Its goal is to do this through its Authenticator app. The authenticator doesn't only use a password, but it uses an additional layer of protection that uses a token or a code to identify a returning user or a device. It is a classic way for users to control their digital identities.

3. Healthcare

The patient, as the central point of the healthcare ecosystem, reserves the right to accurate information. It can also be examined as a matter of life and death. Security and privacy of health data are very important. It helps in tracking the batch numbers and serials of prescription drugs. To store patient data, hospitals have moved away from recordkeeping from paper to blockchain technology which is kept confidential. Would give a number key to the patient to access these records to keep him in control of who can view that data. To track the patient's health history, and patient diagnoses can also be stored.

4. Wills or inheritances

Paper inheritances or wills can now be put back with digital ones, stored, and created using the blockchain network. It must use smart contracts to make someone's document both legally binding and crystal clear as to the other who should receive those assets when a person passes away.

5. Food safety

The interesting use of blockchain technology in food safety can trace food from its origin to our plate. Through the immutable nature of blockchain, the transport of products from their origin to the market can trace. Can trace the source of the contaminant accurately and quickly in the case of food-borne illnesses.

6. Digital voting

Voter fraud has always been a trouble and a great concern, but now it will not be anymore. We can make our vote count with the immutable nature of blockchain technology. The token-based system developed using blockchain technology will secure the system of 'one unchangeable vote per person.' It will make voting transparent and will notify regulators of any changes made to the network.

7. Real estate

Title and ownership details are stored on the blockchain, making it easier to transfer and trace ownership. Eliminating the use of paper from the equation offers a clear picture of legal ownership. Titles are stored and can be viewed on the blockchain network, updated, and altered whenever required.

8. Data sharing

Introduced by IOTA, the IOTA Foundation developed a distributed ledger technology; it involves using the blockchain to sell or share unused data. The unused data bundles of the enterprises could be routed to places that require the most. Blockchain can be used as a platform to store data to upgrade a host of industries.

9. Weapons tracking

Blockchain technology would enable law enforcement and the federal government to track weapon or gun ownership. It will act as a transparent and unchanging registry that will also help record sold weapons privately.

10. Copyright and royalty protection

Copyright and ownership laws on videos, music, blogs, and other online content are essential in today's age. These laws can secure through blockchain technology. Blockchain would also provide authentic and real-time royalty distribution data to musicians and content creators.

11. Equity trading

At some point, blockchain could replace or rival current equity trading platforms to buy and sell stocks. Because blockchain networks settle and validate transactions quickly, it could eliminate the several-day wait time investors encounter when selling stocks and access to their funds for withdrawal or reinvestment

12. Workers' rights

Another important use for blockchain is as a means to strengthen the rights of workers around the globe. According to the International Labor Organization, worldwide, about 25 million people work in forced labor conditions. With the

U.S. State Department, Coca-Cola and other partners are working on a blockchain registry that completes with smart contracts -- protocols that facilitate, verify or enforce a contract, to improve labor policies and pressure employers to honor digital contracts with their workers.

13. Tax regulation and compliance

Let's discussed how important immutability and transparency are yet? For example, marijuana companies can use blockchain to record their sales and show lawmakers that they're abiding by local, federal, and/or state laws. These sales act as a comprehensive record for the IRS that they've paid their share of taxes to the federal government, assuming that they're profitable.

Blockchain technology is an innovation that a majority of people have accepted. Though the features of blockchain are admirable, one should remember that it is not a solution to every problem and that different blockchains will suit several needs and circumstances. The applications of blockchain will broadly vary from one industry to other.

Chapter 5

Investing in Bitcoin

Strategies for investing in Bitcoin

Cryptocurrency has gained significant attraction in recent years and has caused excitement, especially in the investment sector. In the first week of 2021, the price of Bitcoin hit a new record high of $42,000. However, in January, Bitcoin's value dropped by more than 20%, while some other cryptocurrencies continued to fell.

We need to know innovative ways to invest in Bitcoin to stay in this ever-fluctuating market.

The volatile and massive changes in its prices show how unstable the crypto world is. It can get scary, especially if someone is new to the unexplored world of digital currencies. Make some poor initial decisions, and investors could be deep in debt in no time. Following are five smart ways to invest in Bitcoin that will push investors in the right direction.

1. Only Invest That Investor Willing To Lose

Taking financial risks makes some people nervous, while some take complete advantage and move on to a potential opportunity. Advisably, if taking risks makes someone nervous, deeply think before investing in cryptocurrency as it is extremely volatile. However, if the investor is a risk-taker, invest only a portion he is willing to lose if things go south.

People should only invest the amount that they can afford to lose. The primary purpose of investment, be it digital or traditional, is to add more value to existing wealth and not lose it entirely. Therefore, it is one of the wise ways to invest in Bitcoin. This way, even if investors suffer losses, they won't completely strip investors of their wealth and won't be destroyed.

Generally, there is no rule that people should invest the same as some other person did. Just because "A" invested $10,000 doesn't mean the others have to do the same. What matters is that individuals invest within their limit, that is, what they are willing to lose, and this is the smart way to invest in Bitcoin.

2. Maintain A Healthy Crypto Portfolio

A healthy portfolio involves investing in more crypto than just in Bitcoin. This strategy helps to maximize profits and minimize losses. Yes, it also has its complications, but it's profitable than investing in just one coin. In their pricing, cryptocurrencies are extremely volatile.

Diversifying a portfolio by investing in several cryptocurrencies will allow investors to protect themselves from the potential risks involved. People won't get all the benefits of a skyrocketing coin like Bitcoin, but they also won't lose everything if its value drops. By doing this, the investor also won't be too exposed to a single investment. Diversification is one of the intelligent ways to invest in Bitcoin and can help to stabilize gains.

3. Don't Invest in That Based on Hype

Like any other traditional investment, just ignoring the hype and remove the noise regarding Bitcoin will be crucial. When investment in Bitcoins is concerned, our decisions shouldn't be based on that; what others are saying? A wise Bitcoin investor never makes his decisions based on noise and hype as it is precarious. Relying on what others say about Bitcoin is not fruitful at all.

Making money in the market of Bitcoin isn't easy. The price might fall suddenly, leading to a shocking loss. Investors need to have patience and accurate knowledge to make worthwhile profits. It is important to take advice from people who have adequate knowledge about investment and trading strategies, and picking the right people can be challenging. Preferably, to invest in Bitcoin, the smart ways would be to study the market in-depth; the knowledge gained might be used to take calculated risks and ask for guidance from experts if necessary. Doing this will allow investors to form their strategy and successfully separate unwanted hyped-up information.

4. Start Small Investment, Rather Than Big

It is usually wise to keep an individual's initial investment in Bitcoin limited, and it is considered one of the right ways to invest in Bitcoin. People always need to be kept in mind that its price falls and rises compared to other cryptocurrencies. Even the highly experienced investors have invested in Bitcoin, just a single-digit percentage of their capital while investing the rest of capital on less volatile assets.

5. Keep it Safe and Secure

Even today, many crypto exchanges persist in suffering the occasional hack. It is very important to choose crypto with the best security and invest in regular security audits to ensure a highly secured crypto trading platform. As Bitcoin does not exist in any physical form, experienced Bitcoin investors store Bitcoin in digital wallets. A hardware wallet is an offline, handheld device that safely stores the private key compulsory to transfer investor's Bitcoin holdings from one place to other.

Choose a Wallet

When the option to choosing a Bitcoin wallet comes, crypto investors have many options. The first thing they will need to know about crypto wallets is the concept of very useful hot wallets (online wallets) and cold wallets (paper or hardware wallets).

Hot Wallets

Online wallets are known as "hot" wallets. Hot wallets are run only on internet-connected devices like phones, computers, or tablets. Can create weakness because these wallets create the private keys to user coins on these internet-connected devices. In another way, a hot wallet can be very convenient for users to make and access transactions with their assets rapidly. It may sound incredible, but people who are not concerned with security when using hot wallets can have the risk of stealing their funds.

For small amounts of crypto assets, hot wallets are best used for cryptocurrency traders frequently and actively exchange. Traditional financial wisdom would say to have only paying out money in a checking account while the bulk money of a person is in the savings accounts or other investment accounts. The same could be said for hot wallets. Hot wallets include desktop, mobile, web, and exchange account custody wallets.

Exchange wallets are protective accounts offer by the exchanges. In this wallet type, the user is not the private key of the currency held in this hot wallet. If an event occurs and the exchange is hacked, or your account settled, you would lose all your funds. The term "not your key, not your coin" is mostly repeated within cryptocurrency communities and forums

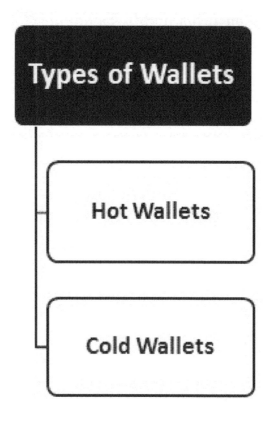

Cold Wallets

The simplest explanation of a cold wallet is as a wallet that is not connected directly to the internet and therefore has a very low risk of being compromised. These wallets can also be called hardware wallets or offline wallets. These wallets store the private key of a user on something which is not directly connected to the internet and use software that works in parallel. In this, the users can view their portfolio without any risk of putting their private key.

The most secure method to store cryptocurrency offline is through a paper wallet. Can generate a paper wallet off of certain websites. It produces both private and public keys that you can print out on paper. In these addresses, accessing cryptocurrency is only possible if you have that paper with the private key. Many people cover these paper wallets and store them at their banks in safety deposit boxes. May safely in their homes because these wallets meant high-security risk and long-term investments, so users cannot quickly trade or sell Bitcoin stored in this way.

A more common type of cold wallet is a hardware wallet. A hardware wallet is a USB drive device that securely stores a user's private key offline. Such wallets have significant advantages over hot wallets as they are safe from viruses that could affect one's computer. Another advantage of a hardware wallet is, the private keys are never in contact with potentially vulnerable software or the user's network-connected computer. These devices are also open sources, allowing the community to control its safety through code audits rather than company state that it is safe to use.

Three things should consider while setting up a wallet: the first is an exchange account of a user to buy and sell, a hot wallet to trade or sell small to medium amounts of crypto, and a cold hardware wallet that stores larger holdings long-term durations.

How to Buy Bitcoin with PayPal

It is also possible to buy Bitcoin via payment processor PayPal. There are two techniques to purchase Bitcoin through PayPal. The most convenient method is to purchase cryptocurrencies using the buyer's PayPal account. The second method uses the buyer's PayPal account balance to purchase a crypto asset from a third-party provider. The second option is not as convenient as the first because a small number of third-party sites allow buyers to purchase Bitcoin using the PayPal button.

Four cryptocurrencies, including Bitcoin, Litecoin, Ethereum, and Bitcoin Cash, can be purchased directly from PayPal.

Set up a cryptocurrency account with PayPal, the following points of information are required: Name, Date of Birth, Physical address, and finally, Tax Identification Number. There are some different ways in which investors can buy Bitcoin through PayPal.

Some of them are:

1. Existing balance in user PayPal account.
2. A debit card linked to use PayPal account
3. Bank account linked to use PayPal account

To purchase Bitcoin using PayPal, it is not possible to use a credit card. PayPal will display a price during the purchase process. However, the built-in volatility of cryptocurrency prices is those prices that are subject to change quickly. Investors should make sure that they have sufficient funds in their accounts to make the purchase.

When buying a Bitcoin from PayPal, it makes money off cryptocurrency spread, the difference between exchange rate USD, and crypto and Bitcoin's market price. For each purchase, the company also charges a transaction fee. These fees depend on the number of dollars purchased. For example, for purchases between $100 to $200, a flat fee of $0.50 is charged. Subsequently, the fee is a percentage of the total amount. For example, for purchases between $100 to $200, 2% of the total amount is charged.

One drawback of purchasing crypto through PayPal is that buyers cannot transfer the cryptocurrency outside the payment processor's platform. So that, it is not possible to transfer cryptocurrencies to an external crypto wallet from

PayPal's wallet.

The other drawback of using PayPal is that very few online traders and exchanges allow payment processors to purchase payment. eToro is the example that allows on its platform the use of PayPal to purchase Bitcoin.

How to Buy Bitcoin with Credit Card

Buying Bitcoin with credit cards is similar to buying crypto with debit cards or automated clearing house (ACH) transfers. The buyer will need to enter his credit card details with the online trading firm or exchange and authorize the transaction. Generally, it is not a good effort to purchase Bitcoin with credit cards. A couple of reasons for this are discussed below.

First, all exchanges, due to the risk of fraud and associated processing fees, didn't allow Bitcoin to use credit cards. Credit card processing can take additional charges on such transactions. Therefore, in addition to paying transaction fees, the buyer will end up with the processing fees that exchange may pass onto the buyer.

The second reason is the purchases through credit cards can be expensive. Credit card issuers act towards Bitcoin purchases as cash advances and demand hefty interest rates and fees on such advances. For example, both American Express and Chase consider purchases of cryptocurrencies transactions as a cash advances. Thus, if someone using an American Express card purchase $100 worth of Bitcoin, he will pay $10 plus 25% of an annual percentage fee.

Purchasing Bitcoin through an indirect method is to get a Bitcoin Rewards credit card. The function of such cards is like buyer's typical rewards credit card excluding they offer rewards in the form of Bitcoin. So, they can invest the cashback into Bitcoin earned from purchases. The BlockFi Bitcoin Rewards Credit Card4 is an example of a Bitcoin Rewards card. Mind out that the annual fee charged on these cards may be high, and there may be additional costs related to the conversion of crypto into fiat currencies.

Alternate Ways of Buying Bitcoin

While exchanges like Binance or Coinbase remain the most popular ways of purchasing Bitcoin. Below are some additional methods Bitcoin owners utilize.

Bitcoin ATMs

Bitcoin ATMs act as in-person Bitcoin exchanges. Individuals can purchase Bitcoin by inserting cash into the machine and then transferred it to a safe digital wallet. In recent years, Bitcoin ATMs have become increasingly popular; Coin ATM radars can help users track down the closest machines

.

P2P Exchanges

Unlike decentralized exchanges, which match up sellers and buyers anonymously and make all aspects of the transaction easy, some peer-to-peer (P2P) exchange services provide a more direct connection between users. An example of such an exchange is Local Bitcoins. After creating an account, an investor can post requests to buy or sell Bitcoin, including basic information about price and payment methods. Users then browse via listings of buy and sell offers and choosing only those trade partners with whom users wish to transact.

How to Sell Bitcoin

A buyer can sell Bitcoin at the same position that he purchased the cryptocurrency, such as peer-to-peer and cryptocurrency exchanges platforms. Typically, selling a Bitcoin on these platforms is the same as the process available to purchase the cryptocurrency.

Depending on the market demand and composition at the venue, the price for Bitcoin offering may vary. For example, the seller may only click a button and identify an order type (i.e., whether should sell the crypto to limit losses or be sold immediately at available prices) to conduct the sale. Crypto exchanges charge a percentage of the cryptocurrency sale amount as fees. For example, Coinbase exchange charges 1.49% as fees of the overall transaction amount.

There are no limits on the sale amount of cryptocurrency. Generally, exchanges have daily or monthly withdrawal limits. Therefore, on a large scale, cash may not be instantly available to the trader.

Before the COVID-19 pandemic, Bitcoin has outstanding long-term price increases. Bitcoin's price has increased all over the place within the years, sometimes jumping by hundreds of dollars in few hours. Given such price changes, Bitcoin has provided investors higher than average returns in exchange for higher than average risk.

From investing in Bitcoins to make a profit, investors have to carry out a deep study. This way, the investor will be more knowledgeable about Bitcoin and understand its utility to the crypto world. In this form of investment, the investor doesn't have to bet to make a profit, then be careful with whatever decisions. The worst thing is to invest in cryptocurrencies that investors about know little or nothing.

Do your research

Focus investing in coins investors believe in and don't mind "bag holding" and use wallets and exchanges that investors are confident in using (starting with Coinbase/Coinbase Pro; that is probably the most beginner-friendly platform an exchange/wallet). To start with the safer and bets Bitcoin, then make way to the top alts like XRP and LTC, then consider the others down the list.

Take some time to understand the history of the market.

Crypto markets work 24/7. Significant price action happens in early AM when the volume is low. Sometimes crypto goes up 400%, and sometimes it goes down 80%, sometimes a coin's value does nothing for a month. Good luck telling you which events are coming next. If an investor comes in during a period when things are up, he may consider it will always be like this, but it has never been the case. Sometimes Bitcoin is up, and altcoins are down; sometimes altcoins look like they will have influence, sometimes everything is down, sometimes everything is up, etc. Rarely everything will be up, but when it is, that period is not long-lasting. Investors must be ready for the mood swings. Only experience and/or research will prepare them for the many possible phases of Bitcoin.

Be conservative and cautious.

If people keep their investment reasonable and slowly enter the market over time, they will remove many day-to-day stresses. Reasonable access limits their crypto investments to 1% – 4% of their investable capital and limits buy-ins to no more than 10% of that.

Have a long view of the market.

Don't focus too much on what the trend is now. Instead, try to pick an investment and strategy, stick to it, and keep a long view of the market. People are either going to trade, invest, or both. If they are investing, try to limit their trading and focus too much on dollar rates. If they are trading, pay attention to their dollar rates and don't go at the top into HODL mode.

Be wary of your emotions.

Sometimes our emotions will almost lose our money. The only exception is when we luck out, and FOMO buys the lowest or sells the top. Always rely on data, never listen to heart, gut, or anything else that can't be formulated based entirely on data.

Start small

Start investing with a very small amount of money and slowly increase it once buyers know everything is working. This advice is used to send money between exchanges, trading, testing a bot or TA strategy, sending money between peers, etc.

Be aware of the tax implications and regulations

There are very complex tax rules and limited regulations. Nothing inconvenient if we prepare in advance, but nothing can be ignored either. As a rule of thumb, if it is questionable (buying stuff on the dark web, online gambling, not paying taxes, etc.), it is always questionable in the crypto world.

Be aware of the trend

An investor will do much better if he can tell the difference between a bear market and a bull market.

Techniques to earn money with Bitcoin.

Let's discuss the methods by which we can earn a good amount of money with Bitcoin? More importantly, beginners who are looking to make great profits with bitcoin should prefer trading Bitcoin. In this process, traders have to buy Bitcoin when the price goes down and then sell at a higher price to earn great profits with great margins. Beginners must succeed in bitcoin trading; for this, they learn some useful strategies and tips that help them get profits most of the time. Beginners have to choose the right platform to obtain better services such as low fees or charges, customer support, and useful features.

Following are the main and simple techniques by which everyone can easily get a good amount of money and also plenty of benefits with the cryptocurrency.

1. Trading

Trading is a primary way to make a profit, and it feels like icing on the cake as it is accessible the whole day trading Bitcoin. Individuals have to exchange their digital currency into local currency by using a professional website. Also, check the situation and charts of the market on which the whole process is based. Significantly trade enough amount that you can afford if by chance you lose it.

2. Investing

The technique is that one knows when is the good time to sell bitcoins because this technique plays a crucial role. If an investor wants to invest his money for the long-term, it is recommended to keep their bitcoins in a hardware wallet.

3. Mining

It is the process of placing new blocks to the blockchain of bitcoin by solving cryptographic puzzles that also assist in earning a great profit. The best thing about cloud mining services is that users have to pay once only; users neither have to mine nor worry about increasing electricity bills. After investing in cloud mining services, they constantly receive their share.

4. Micro earning

It is easy to understand conducting different kinds of micro earning tasks is the way of earning money. It can be done by accomplishing online surveys and also by watching advertisement videos. There are different micro earning sites that grant users minimal bitcoins. Further, micro earnings sites are the place to join instantly; users should also know about the bonus method.

5. Accept as a payment option

Now, every single person increases bitcoin by considering BTC as a payment option. If someone is a dealer or thinking to be, it would be the top choice to bring together bitcoin in his payment ecosystem. When he completely accept bitcoin as his payment method, it opens all doors to earn profit. At the same time, users can accept payments anywhere they are.

6. Lending

Without creating any hurdle, bitcoin also generates huge money for its users. Individuals can render bitcoins on lease to, and they can fill their account because holding BTC in a locker cannot increase the money. Furthermore, if they want to avoid spam? Then they must have their bitcoins with an original lending platform. When choosing a trustworthy platform, put their bitcoins into it and enjoy benefits of interest.

Finally, these are the popular techniques by which users can simply and easily earn a lot of money with bitcoin. Also, apart from this, by making a wise investment in BTC, investors can enjoy several benefits, as well as it helps them in growing their business. To earn more profits, investors can also enter the BTC trading market.

Top 10 Risks Of Bitcoin Investing (How To Avoid Them)

Today Bitcoin is the most successful currency, but there are bound to be some problems with any new limit. Regardless of bitcoin's recent popularity, there are some serious risks when it points to investing in cryptocurrency.

With so many people hurry to invest, it's important to be conscious of the BTC market's concerns. Following are the top 10 risks of investing in bitcoin and how to avoid them.

1. Young Technology

Cryptocurrency is quite a very young technology. Bitcoin came about ten years ago, and it has so far developed into something solid. With so many changes in the past few years, there's no significant information on how the market will evolve. Bitcoin may become useless in the future. The best means to approach this investment opportunity is with due diligence and caution. People take steps to secure their funds and brace them for the future of the market.

2. Currency Or Investment Opportunity?

Cryptocurrency could be a productive online currency exchange; however, investors buy up bitcoins to invest more than stocks. Some investors even think that for retirement, Bitcoin is a solid investment opportunity. With a constantly moving market, zero physical collateral, and no regulation, investors can lose everything they invest. While Bitcoin could pay off, caution is the best way to approach this investment. Small steps and small investments will cover more ground.

3. Financial Loss

Bitcoin sometimes has been referred to as a Ponzi scheme. As more people buy Bitcoin, it creates a fantasy in people and a bubble economy. When the bubble bursts, bitcoin will become useless; many people hold cryptocurrency but cannot sell it. If there is no return on the investment, that can equal a painful financial loss.

4. Limited Use

Bitcoin may move toward a new monetary exchange; although, some companies accept Bitcoin as a viable form of currency. Currently, a small number of online stores, including Newegg and Monoprix, Overstock, allow crypto exchanges. Additionally, Bitcoin holders can use their reserves for travel with companies like Air Lituanica, AirBaltic, and CheapAir.com. Unfortunately, most companies do not accept Bitcoin as a legal exchange.

5. Block Withholding

New Bitcoins created by solving mathematical equations are called "blocks," which can be created whenever a Bitcoin exchange is online. Mine a block, a mining pool use computational power and hides it instead of reporting that new block to the network. Essentially, this is a way to select a few to get the benefits, while others leave with nothing.

6. Technology Reliance

Bitcoin is an online exchange that is dependent on technology. Coins are mined digitally, exchanged through a smart wallet, and kept in checking using various systems. Without technology, the significance of cryptocurrency is nothing. Unlike other forms of investment or currency, there is no physical guarantee to back it up. With gold, bonds, mutual funds, real estate, people own something possible to be exchanged. With a technology-based currency, Bitcoin owners are more at risk of cyber threats, online frauds and operated with a system that can shut down.

7. Little Or No Regulation

Currently, there are no proper regulations for operating the Bitcoin market. The government doesn't have a clear viewpoint on cryptocurrency; the market is too new. It is not even taxed, which can make it attractive as an investment opportunity. Therefore, a lack of taxation could create problems should Bitcoin result in competition for government currency. Hence, cryptocurrency is not a broadly accepted currency, but the future may be ever-changing.

8. Fraud

With hacking, there is a chance of fraud in the bitcoin market. Buyers and sellers are considering trading bitcoins online, but some exchanges can be a forgery as long as their rise in popularity. The Securities and Exchange Commission and the Consumer Finance Protection Bureau warn against these transactions where unsuspicious investors are deceived out of their Bitcoins in deceitful exchanges. This low security creates a high risk for investors. Although systems have been created to act toward these problems, security remains a big issue.

9. Cybertheft

As we know, cryptocurrency is technology-based, which keeps this investment open to cyberattacks. Exchanges are often hacked -- even if users have the defense of a smart wallet. Hacking is a genuine risk since there is no way to recover a person's stolen or lost bitcoins. Additionally, if the user has a wallet and forgets or misplaces his key, there is sometimes a way to recover his coins.

10. The Volatile And Fluctuating Market

The price of bitcoin is all the time changing. One bitcoin was worth $6,461.01 as of November 6, 2018. If a buyer purchased a bitcoin on December 17, 2017, the price exceeded $20,000. Later that, on the 24th, buyers sell their investment for about $14,626. The bitcoin market is constantly flowing back and forth. There's an uncertainty with such an uncertain market if the investor will return on his investment. To avoid a huge loss, keep an attentive eye on the market.

Investing in Cryptocurrency for Long-Term Gain

Compared with traditional stocks, cryptocurrencies are volatile and need investors to prepare themselves for all types of scenarios. FOMO buying and Panic selling always don't help in the long run, and with how irregular the market movements are, it can help things become smooth by looking at the bigger picture.

Will Bitcoin appreciate long-term?

Bitcoin has a fixed supply of 21 million BTC, paid to miners for securing the network. After every four years or so, halved the supply rate, making Bitcoin more scarce with time.

With this kind of periodic supply rate reduction, BTC isn't the only cryptocurrency. Many other altcoins also follow this depreciating supply schedule. Since a limited number of Bitcoin will ever exist, even lost coins donate to the asset's shortage.

Cryptocurrencies provide an impressive value scheme in which investors can invest small amounts and gain huge profits, but it doesn't mean that there isn't any risk involved. In reality, most investors minimize risk by expanding their portfolios into many assets.

Should I invest in altcoins?

Altcoin investments are known as Grayscale Investments, one of the world's most leading institutional investors in the blockchain arena, with a portfolio containing multiple cryptocurrencies, including Bitcoin, Litecoin, Ethereum, XRP, and Stellar, among others.

Its portfolio is primarily has a hold of Bitcoin, which accounts for more than $6 billion of the total AUM $7.3 billion, but owning a mix of Bitcoin and other altcoins is a solid place to start. More people are investing huge amounts into the first cryptocurrency than altcoins like Litecoin and XRP.

Whenever an altcoin crashes, earnings from Bitcoin or altcoins may save an investor's portfolio's worth. Mostly altcoin investors move their funds into Bitcoin once it starts to come back, pushing Bitcoin even more up while altcoins decrease in value.

How risky is it?

The crypto market is unpredictable and creates millionaires as often as it bankrupts. There's objectively no risk-free way to invest in anything, and only experience and intuition will help people walk away victorious. How much people should invest depends on how much they are willing to lose, and that should give them a fair idea regarding the level of risk engaged in entering the cryptocurrency world.

Unlike the traditional stock market, there are no more or any centralized entities to hold accountable here. For running scams, this makes the blockchain industry perfect, and it is critical to only invest in projects that a person thinks are genuinely valuable.

Just because a rise in an asset's value doesn't mean it is worth anything. From blatant pump and dump schemes to fraudulent ICOs, there's a lot to learn and understand about crypto markets better. We can't capitalize on any project if we can't identify its value.

Where can I buy cryptocurrencies?

Digital assets can be purchased, sold, and in few cases, stored on different crypto exchanges on the web. Two main types of exchanges are centralized and decentralized exchanges.

The simple approach

The function of Centralized exchanges is in the same way as traditional exchanges facilitate trading. To collect bid and ask data and then match traders in real-time, an order book is used for all this. The price of an asset is calculated through the demand/supply ratio on the order book.

An alternative technical approach

Decentralized exchanges encountered multiple iterations over the last decade. With DEXs, attempts to use an order book system have issued slow exchanges with little liquidity. There is a lack of rewards or incentives for market makers. As the Automated Market Makers (AMMs) introduced, modern DEXs threaten some established Cass. Alternatively, using an order book to track bid/ask, current DEXs lock pairs of tokens in liquidity pools. In the pool, the ratio of tokens determines their price, and for contributing and staking to the pool's liquidity, liquidity providers are rewarded.

Kriptomat provides a desktop account and mobile app with an easy-to-use interface for storing, buying, and selling cryptocurrency securely.

What kind of exchange should I use?

There are many pros and cons to both types of exchanges. Different from DEXs, centralized exchanges are dependably fast, with different teams of dedicated experts operating to improve the platform for the possible experience.

Additionally, CEXs are big targets for hacks; they are also more likely to compensate users for losses than an exchange without any central authority. Many CEOs also have built-in to exchange fiat currency for crypto on-ramps, but some decentralized exchanges also offer this feature.

Where should I store my digital assets?

Another critical facet of long-term investment in the crypto asset is storage. Although exchange wallets are almost secure, leaving investor's assets online is a risk that's quite simple to diminish. Whether it's extra phone users, have lying around or a hardware wallet, storing their assets offline is pretty easy and more secure to set up.

Ensure to store the user's wallet address' seed phrase, so they always have access to their tokens. Forget this information can decrease the entire portfolio's value because their assets are not accessible.

What kind of cryptocurrencies are there?

Many altcoins are available to purchase. Stablecoins offer cryptocurrency adaptability with the stability of fiat currency. For example, Tether (USDT) is a famous stablecoin with its value fixed to the U.S. dollar. This lets traders enter or exit markets at a moment's notice can't wait for fiat-to-crypto transformation.

The facts suggest that there are about 5,000 altcoins in existence, but they are not worth money, and many of them probably aren't worth time. Although, the dollar value of the altcoin isn't always relative to how valuable it is.

Many tokens are more beneficial for the services they provide than their inherent value. It's easy to get lost in trend lines and technical indicators, but it's critical to invest in only genuine projects that can give value to the market in early projects.

Impossible claims often just remain impossible. Before investing a part of their portfolio in cryptocurrencies, investors do their research and avoid anything that even slightly seems like a multi-level crypto marketing scheme.

What cryptocurrencies should I invest in long-term?

Most customers decide to stick with the top coins by market capitalization for long-term investments, just like BTC, ETH, and XRP, and others were seen on the cryptocurrency prices table. It will give users a good idea of what the market generally thinks is more valuable and is an excellent means to dip their feet into the sphere of blockchain technology.

New projects will enter the top rankings just rapidly they leave, and by the market, this testing can be useful in determining what's precious and what's garbage. It can be attractive to invest huge amounts in high-risk assets, but this can be destroyed, especially for long-term investors.

How do I know if a cryptocurrency is worth investing in?

Investing in anything begs analysis. For long-term proceedings, investors use three major methods to measure the upside and risk of a particular asset. The fundamental analysis estimates a project's or intrinsic token value in the market situation and its outlook.

Before a token sale, most projects publish a whitepaper, and studying this document may present more profound insight into what the asset offers. Make sure to view economic factors and other industry-specific circumstances like Bitcoin's supply halving after every four years.

What other forms of analysis can We use?

Another famous method of evaluation is via technical analysis. Involves examining historical price chart data to find patterns in the market's behavior. It May help understand trader's behavior, and cases like prominent support, resistance levels, daily trading volume, and certain technical indicators can explain a broader picture of its prospective potential.

Although technical analysis is sometimes reserved for short-term projects, it's possible to learn how it behaves to external events by indicating patterns in the price chart assets. It can be beneficial in the long-term and, join with fundamental analysis, can give a rounded idea of a project's value.

With quantitative analysis, investors can measure how well an asset is likely to execute based on historical data. Of future appreciation, past performance is never indicative, and it's critical to learn more, not just about the token but the market investing in it.

How can I profit from cryptocurrencies?

The whole purpose of any investment is to make money, and crypto investments can make investor's money work in many ways. Created as a solution to the expandability and consumption of energy issues with Bitcoin's Proof-of-Work breakthrough, Proof-of-Stake has crawled into many blockchain-based projects over the last couple of years.

Instead of satisfying miners for running calculations to validate transactions, Proof-of-Stake facilitates stakers by locking tokens into a smart contract to provide liquidity. Depending on the token, rewards cover a range from variable APR on the staked token to completely new tokens that can further stake.

Decentralized Finance (DeFi) is called a hotbed for staking protocols. In the last year, hacks have led to millions evacuated from various DeFi platforms – not exactly where we want our life savings. Some staking executions allow network contributors to delegate their stake for validator nodes, balancing risk and security.

Others offer rewards for fixed periods in case merely holding assets in their wallets. This facility to stake offline then a hardware wallet makes things more attractive for long-term investors, offering security from spiteful actors on the network.

The most realistic approach to profiting long-term projects for most people may be collecting a diversified portfolio of crypto assets and periodically re-balancing the portfolio.

Is staking more profitable than mining?

For individual investors, staking isn't just beneficial. It has led to a sign of people entering the crypto sphere, lowering the hurdle for entry from high-end mining machines to a normal hardware wallet.

Though most of the cryptocurrency mining business has moved to feasible energy sources, Proof-of-Stake is more environmentally friendly and energy-efficient.

It also makes 51% of attacks harder to accomplish due to the utter cost of attaining that much more authority. Miners also have to act toward the value of their machines' periodic hardware upgrades, depreciation over time and accommodating other running costs of mining the network.

What is the future of cryptocurrencies?

Cryptocurrency investments gain impressive growth in short periods, but it's beneficial to have a detailed understanding of how a project works before taking the risk of any capital. Short-term investments are an easy way to make a quick buck, but trading on shorter time scales requires intuition, experience, and nuance.

Volatile markets can discourage all kinds of emotions in less-experienced traders, and the right decision at the right moment can often turn out harmful in the grand scheme of things. Blockchain empowers the individual investor and takes control apart from centralized institutions. Bitcoin gave us a decentralized economy, and along with this, altcoins gave us a decentralized economy.

Although the industry is young, it's already on the road to ordinary adoption. As more people are ready to get, cryptocurrencies may soon become more of an investment in the future economy and less investment in blockchain.

Cryptocurrency vs. Traditional Investments

Although cryptocurrency is a new technology, the nature of investing in it doesn't vary tremendously from currencies or traditional stocks. Like any investment, investors are accepting a certain amount of risk in hopes of earning a return.

However, cryptocurrency remains a greater risk than stocks. The whole point of cryptocurrency is to persist unregulated by any regulatory body or single government, but this helps increase volatility. Furthermore, we need to consider other facts, like storage and cybersecurity.

Cryptocurrency investments are not accessible through traditional brokerages. Investors need to use a cryptocurrency trading platform to avail themselves. Likewise, they cannot invest in tax-advantaged accounts like RRSP or TFSA, which means that they need to be responsible for their income taxes on their investment gains.

Chapter 6

Bitcoin Mining

What is Bitcoin Mining?

Bitcoin mining refers to the process of adding transaction data to Bitcoin's public ledger of previous transactions or blockchain. This ledger of previous transactions is called the blockchain or, as it is a chain of blocks—the blockchain work to confirm transactions as having taken place to the rest of the network.

Bitcoin nodes use the blockchain to differentiate permissible Bitcoin transactions from attempts to re-spend crypto coins that already have been spent elsewhere.

Bitcoin mining is executed by solving complex computational math puzzles through high-powered computers; these puzzles are so complicated that they cannot be solved by hand and complicated adequately to tax even unbelievably powerful computers. The result of bitcoin mining is twofold. First, when computers solve these complicated math puzzles on the bitcoin network, they create new bitcoin. And second, by solving complex math problems, bitcoin miners verifying its transaction information make the bitcoin payment network secure and trustworthy.

When an individual sends bitcoin anywhere, this process is called a transaction. Transactions made online, or in-store are documented by physical receipts, banks, and point-of-sale systems. Bitcoin miners reach the same thing by binding transactions together in "blocks" and add them to a public record called the "blockchain." Records of those blocks then maintain by Nodes so that they can be further verified into the future.

Whenever bitcoin miners build a new block of transactions to the blockchain, make sure that those transactions are accurate, this is a part of their job. Furthermore, bitcoin miners also make sure that bitcoin is not duplicated; a unique fact of digital currencies is called "double-spending." With printed currencies, forgery is always an issue. But generally, once someone spends $20 at the store, the bill is in the clerk's hands. However, it's a different story with digital currency.

Is Bitcoin Mining still profitable?

Bitcoin mining can be profitable for some individuals and still make sense. Equipment is easily obtained, although, from not many hundred dollars up to about $10,000, competitive ASICs cost anywhere. To stay competitive in the market, we have adapted some machines. For example, some hardware to lower energy requirements allows users to alter settings, lowering costs. Potential miners to understand their breakeven price should do a cost/benefit analysis before producing the fixed-cost purchases of the equipment. The parameters needed to make this calculation are:

Cost of power/electricity

What is the user's electricity rate? Users can find this information on their electric bill measured in kWh. Keep in mind that rates may change depending on the time of day, the season, and other factors.

Efficiency

How much power does the user's system consume, measured in watts?

Time

What is the expected time user will spend in mining?

Bitcoin value

What is the value of one bitcoin in another official currency or U.S. dollars?

There are many web-based profitability calculators, such as the one provided by CryptoCompare; through this, miners can examine the cost/benefit equation. These calculators are distinct slightly, and few are more complex than others.

Run investor's analysis often using different price levels for both the value of bitcoins and the cost of power. Also, to see how that impacts the analysis changed the level of difficulty. Determine that at what price level bitcoin mining will become profitable for the user—that is user's breakeven price. As of May 2020, the bitcoin price is hovering about $8,000. For a completed block given a current reward of 6.25 BTC, miners are rewarded about $50,000 after completing a hash. Be sure, as the bitcoin price is highly variable, this reward figure may likely change.

Can reduce the difficulty in mining and increase the speed, place profitability in reach. To compete against the mega-mining centers, users can join a mining pool, a set of miners who share the rewards and work together. As cost and difficulty have increased, more individual miners have chosen to participate in a pool. The overall reward decreases because it is shared between multiple participants; the way to combine computing power is that mining pools have a greater chance of completing a hashing problem first to receive a reward.

Whether bitcoin mining is still profitable, to answer this question, to run a cost-benefit analysis, we may use a web-based profitability calculator. We can plug in different numbers and find our breakeven point (after that, mining is profitable). Determine if individuals are willing to spend the necessary beginning capital for the hardware and estimate the level of difficulty and the future value of bitcoins. When mining difficulty and declining bitcoin prices, it usually means more ease in receiving bitcoins and fewer miners. When mining difficulty and bitcoin prices rise, contradictory, more miners take part for few bitcoins.

How to mine bitcoin?

Although it is challenging and sometimes profitable, Bitcoin mining is still practicable. While will gained the best results from participating in a mining pool, should consider the following steps to proceed into Bitcoin mining:

Calculate profitability

The primary expenses will include mining hardware and the cost of electricity. Primarily any profit will be based on Bitcoin's value, which is very volatile.

Get mining hardware

Once early calculations are made, think to spend from several hundred dollars to several thousand dollars on mining hardware.

Choose mining software

Next, users need a platform from which they can access the blockchain and manage their mining. There are several popular Bitcoin mining software.

Install a Bitcoin wallet

When users have mined bitcoins, they will need a place to store them; this is called a Bitcoin wallet. Digital wallets let store their bitcoins in "the cloud" but are commonly targeted by cybercriminals. Offline wallets stores bitcoins in a device that is not connected with the internet, offering to add up security.

Enter a mining pool

Joining or entering a mining pool offers a significant chance of success.

Get started

Completing the previous steps, we can start mining, equipment or process should routinely check to ensure everything is working properly.

Bitcoin is an autonomous system of digital money. It has no direct connection to any real-world currency, nor is it controlled by any centralized entity or government.

To operate these transactions securely, miners take participation to solve mathematically complicated problems. The miners who successfully solve those problems add a block to the blockchain and receive a reward of 6.25 bitcoins. As in November 2020, one bitcoin was worth more than $18,000—that means every successful miner gets more than $100,000 worth of Bitcoin, is not only the reward of the miner's effort but the process of mining is generated new bitcoins and is introduced into the flow.

All mining starts with the blockchain. Blockchain is an online ledger that records all the transactions throughout a network. A group of accepted transactions is called a "block." These blocks are then tied together to generate a "chain," hence called a "blockchain."

Requires extensive computational and electrical power in the Bitcoin network, the miner aims to add up individual blocks to the blockchain by solving mathematical problems. At the same time, many miners participate in adding each block; the miner who solves the issue will now add the block, along with approved transactions, to the blockchain. This miner gets a reward of 6.25 bitcoins (as of November 2020).

Due to the difficulty in mining bitcoins, there are different requirements for the basic mining process.

What do I need to mine Bitcoins?

Bitcoin is designed to regulate the difficulty needed to mine one block every 14 days (or after 2,016 blocks mined). The comprehensive goal is to maintain the one bitcoin time required to mine to 10 minutes. Since Bitcoin has been around since 2009, its mining problems are massive; the reason is that resource-intensive and powerful hardware is compulsory to mine.

The most important part required to mine bitcoin is specialized mining hardware called application-specific integrated circuits, or ASICs. The cost of a new ASIC device is anywhere from a few hundred dollars to $10,000. But the cost of mining hardware is only a tiny part of the expense involved. ASICs consume large amounts of electricity, the cost of which can rapidly increase the cost of the device using it.

Users also need to choose mining software to join the Bitcoin network, which isn't as expensive as hardware. Several reliable software options are accessible for free.

Must include all the expenses to decide the profitability of Bitcoin mining: electricity, hardware, and software. The value of Bitcoin, which consistently changes, must also be considered into account and taxes miners might pay.

How much will it cost to mine a bitcoin?

The sudden rise in the price of Bitcoin and most other cryptocurrencies in 2020 has buyers flocking to collect coins at sky-high prices. On the other hand, cryptocurrency miners want to get their coins for free.

But any knowledgeable investor knows there's no free thing when it comes to investing, and mining cryptocurrency is a pricey attempt. According to Buy Bitcoin Worldwide, trying to mine a bitcoin on a computer without specialized hardware will only get a miner about 1 cent value of bitcoin per month. Specialized equipment, such as the Antminer S9 or the Antminer S7, anywhere can cost from a few hundred dollars to thousands of dollars.

Once an investor has forked over the big bucks for mining hardware, little successful mining profits will be moderately offset by the cost of electricity required to operate the devices. According to the CryptoCompare website, mining bitcoin at a rate of about 4,730 GH/s and cost power is 12 cents per KW/h would consume over $111.72 electricity every month and of $1,359.20 each year.

Bitcoin mining becomes more expensive and more difficult by the day. The problem in mining a bitcoin automatically adjusts the hash rate of the miners to make sure the rate of one block after every 10 minutes. With so many professional and competing miners for a limited number of bitcoins, it can be crucial for a non-professional independent miner to achieve much of anything.

Chapter 7

Different Kinds of Altcoins

Ethereum

What is Ethereum?

Ethereum, as a blockchain network, is a decentralized public ledger recording for and verifying transactions. The network users can publish, monetize, create, and use applications on the platform and use its cryptocurrency as payment.

Ethereum is a decentralized, open-source blockchain with smart contract functionality. Ether is a native cryptocurrency of the crypto platform. It is the largest cryptocurrency by market capitalization after Bitcoin and now is the most actively used blockchain. As of May 2021, Ethereum as a cryptocurrency is second in market value only after Bitcoin.

Ethereum was launched in 2013 by programmer Vitalik Buterin. Crowdfunded development in 2014, and the crypto network went live on July 30, 2015. The platform permitted developers to deploy immutable and permanent decentralized applications onto it, through which users can interact. Decentralized finance (DeFi) applications offer a broad arrangement of financial services without the need of any typical financial intermediaries, such as exchanges, banks, or brokerages, allowing users to lend them out for interest or borrow against their holdings. Ethereum also allows for the exchange and creation of NFTs, which are non-interchangeable tokens connected to real-world items or other digital works of art and sold as a unique digital property. Furthermore, many other cryptocurrencies on top of the Ethereum blockchain operate as ERC-20 tokens and have utilized this platform for initial coin offerings.

History of Ethereum

Initially, Ethereum was described by Vitalik Buterin in a white paper, a co-founder and programmer of Bitcoin Magazine, to establish decentralized applications in late 2013. Buterin argued that blockchain technology and Bitcoin could benefit from other applications other than money and that application development needed a scripting language that could connect real-world assets, such as property and stocks, to the blockchain. In 2013, Buterin shortly worked with eToro (another type of cryptocurrency) CEO Yoni Assia on the Colored Coins project and drew up its white paper outlining extra use cases for blockchain technology. Anyway, after failing to acquire agreement on how the project should begin, he proposed to him the development of a new platform as a more general scripting language that would, in the end, become Ethereum.

The Etherium was explicitly designed to be used within the Ether network. But, like Bitcoin, Etherium is now used as an accepted form of payment by some service vendors and merchants. Shopify, Overstock, and CheapAir are the online sites that accept Etherium as payment.

How is Ethereum similar to Bitcoin?

Ethereum is similar to Bitcoin in the sense that they both are cryptocurrencies, decentralized, digital currencies. Another similarity between the two digital currencies is that they both work using the proof-of-work consensus. This means that for both Bitcoin and Ethereum, the confirmation and verification of transactions need a network-wide consensus of nodes. Due to this setup, when it comes to transaction processing, both of them are slow.

Ethereum is moderately faster than Bitcoin: it typically processes 10 to 15 transactions per second, while Bitcoin process 3 to 5 transactions per second. Anyhow, this is true about the current version of Ethereum. One of the important expectations right now in the market is that the upcoming 2.0 upgrade version, among other things, will provide faster transactions.

But the central point that distinct Ethereum from Bitcoin is the smart contracts, the term most closely linked with Ethereum blockchain. Smart contracts are digital contracts that have many applications.

Without going in-depth on Ethereum 2.0, it makes sense to discuss the Beacon chain, which is used to offer an enhancement to Ethereum's features. Beacon chain makes use of a proof-of-stake consensus algorithm instead of proof-of-work; this means that to process transactions, it uses tokens rather than traditional computational power.

Regarding price stability, it is clear that over Ethereum, Bitcoin has a lead. The BTC rate is a major point defining the entire crypto market picture. And the two currencies positively correspond; when Bitcoin falls or rises, the same happens to Ethereum. Bitcoin capture around four times high market capitalization so that it is less unstable in its price.

As far as trading crypto assets is concerned, at the CEX.IO exchange, we observed that in December 2020, Etherium to USD trading volumes grew by 20%, while Bitcoin to USD grew by 47.5%. Due to the rally, Bitcoin became too "expensive" to fund trading strategies and risky to trade. It also shows that ETH is no longer chasing Bitcoin's price changes as nearly as it used to, and this separation may become apparent in the future. We believe that it may act as a psychological trait for users.

Dogecoin

What is Dogecoin?

Dogecoin is a cryptocurrency developed by Billy Markus and Jackson Palmer. Software engineers decided as a joke to create a payment system, making fun of the wild conjecture in cryptocurrencies. Apart from its mocking nature, some consider it a legal investment prospect. Dogecoin characteristics the face of the Shiba Inu dog from the "Doge" meme as its namesake and logo. It was first introduced on December 6, 2013, and abruptly evolve its online community on May 5, 2021, succeeding a market capitalization of US$85,314,347,523. Dogecoin.com promotes the cryptocurrency as a "fun and friendly internet currency", specifying its origins as a joke.

Elon Musk often mentions or talks about Dogecoin currency on his Twitter account, increasing its popularity an outstanding amount in recent years.

Dogecoin is also a cryptocurrency that operating on blockchain technology, similar to Ethereum and Bitcoin. Blockchain is an easily distributed, secure digital ledger that stores all transactions generated using a decentralized digital currency.

All holders hold an identical copy of the blockchain ledger, which with all new transactions in the Doge currency, is frequently updated. Like other cryptocurrencies, Dogecoin's blockchain uses cryptography to keep all transactions safe and secure.

Miners use computers to solve complicated mathematical equations to generate transactions and keep records on the Dogecoin blockchain; this is called the "proof of work" system. In exchange for supporting the blockchain ledger and processing transactions, miners can earn additional Dogecoin, which they can further hold or sell on the open market.

Dogecoin may use for purchases and payments, but it's not still a very effective store of value. Because there is no fixed lifetime cap on the number of Dogecoins generated by mining, meaning that the Dogecoin is highly inflationary. The blockchain rewards miners for work by generating millions of new Dogecoins, making it challenging for price gains in Dogecoins cryptocurrency to hold up.

Dogecoin History

Found initially as a joke, Dogecoin was created by Billy Markus, the IBM software engineer and an Adobe software engineer named Jackson Palmer. They desire to create a peer-to-peer digital currency that could extend a broader demographic than Bitcoin. Furthermore, they wanted to separate it from the contentious history of other coins. On December 6, 2013, Dogecoin was officially launched, and within 30 days, over one million visitors visit Dogecoin.com.

Palmer is attributed to making this idea a reality. At the time, in Sydney, he was a member of the Adobe Systems marketing department. Palmer had added a splash screen after purchasing the domain of Dogecoin.com, which featured the scattered Comic Sans text and coin's logo. After seeing the site, Markus reached out to Palmer and started efforts to develop the currency. Markus designed a Dogecoin protocol on existing cryptocurrencies like Luckycoin and Litecoin, which use scrypt technology in the proof-of-work algorithm. The use of the term scrypt includes that miners or users cannot use SHA-256 Bitcoin mining equipment, and instead of that must use dedicated ASIC and FPGA devices for mining which are known as more complex to produce.

On December 19, 2013, Dogecoin increased nearly 300 % in value in just three days, rising from US$0.00026 to $0.00095, with a capacity of billions of Dogecoins per day. This rise of Dogecoin occurred when many other cryptocurrencies and Bitcoin were reeling from China's decision to ban Chinese banks from investing in the bitcoin economy. After three days, Dogecoin faces its first major crash by decreasing 80% due to this occurrence and large mining pools abusing at the time to mine Dogecoin the small amount of computing power required.

On December 25, 2013, the first massive theft of Dogecoin occurred when were stolen millions of coins during a hack on the cryptocurrency platform Dogewallet. The hacker accessed the platform's filesystem and changes its send and receive page to send any or all crypto coins to a static address. After its breach to help those who lost their funds on Dogewallet, the Dogecoin community took the initiative named "SaveDogemas" to help donate coins to those who had them stolen. After one month, enough money was donated by the dogecoin community to cover the stolen coins.

The trading volume of Dogecoin in January 2014 briefly exceed that of Bitcoin and all other cryptocurrencies. However, its market capitalization remained entirely behind that of Bitcoin. Initially, Dogecoin promoting a randomized reward that can receive after each mining block.

In 2015, co-founder Jackson Palmer left the crypto community and had no plans to return. He was representing Dogecoin as a copper and silver token, minted in 2014 by ShibeMint. Sold these tokens were with private keys. During the 2017 to 2018 cryptocurrency bubble, reaching its total market capitalization of about USD 2 billion, Dogecoin peaked at $0.017/coin on January 7, 2018.

On May 4, 2021, the value of Dogecoin crossed the symbolic hurdle of $0.50, a greater than 20,000% increase in 1 year.

The rise of Dogecoin

Despite its jokey origins, the rise of Dogecoin in 2020 has been seen. DOGE's trading volume now classifies it in the same category as Ethereum and Bitcoin and has entered the top four coins by market cap this year. Currently, it is the sixth most valuable cryptocurrency.

According to data obtained by Crypto Parrot trading simulator, In May Third most-traded cryptocurrency, DOGE was the largest digital asset exchange Binance with a volume of about $116 billion. Ethereum recorded the highest trading volume at $191 billion, followed by Bitcoin at $188 billion.

DOGE also ranked third with a trading volume of $51billion; on the Huobi crypto exchange, Bitcoin ranked second by just $13billion. Ethereum also topped with a volume of $85billion. DOGE, fluctuating cryptocurrency market also based on a meme, is currently valued at about $43billion with a 34 cents token value.

Following a sudden rise to 69c promoted by Tesla entrepreneur Elon Musk. Who valued the currency at about $90bn? It has declined dramatically in the last month. Musk, also CEO of SpaceX, in recent weeks has tweeted that he is "working with Doge to improve the efficiency of the system transaction", classifying the currency as "potentially promising". He has also announced that SpaceX's next mission is to the moon funded by cryptocurrency Dogecoin, a development that offers the crypto its first intimidating utility. Litecoin

What is Litecoin?

Litecoin (LTC) is an open-source software project and a peer-to-peer cryptocurrency released under the license of MIT/X11. Starting in October 2011, Litecoin was an early bitcoin derivative or altcoin. Technically, Litecoin is similar to Bitcoin.

Litecoin creator Charlie Lee sometimes refers to the cryptocurrency as "silver to Bitcoin's gold." Aside from sharing the same codebase, both also exhibit similar price movements in cryptocurrency markets, falling and rising in tandem.

Bitcoin and Litecoin also complement each other. Bitcoin's mandate was to become a means for the daily transaction. But the problem is scaling, which prevented it from completing that role. Meanwhile, Litecoin has picked up the incorporated and mantle scaling technologies into its sphere to enable digital payments on its platform. In 2017, Litecoin had, as some analysts called it, a phenomenal year. The similarities between the two digital currencies might seem mysterious to observers, especially as long as the cryptocurrency ecosystem is assumed to have variations in applications.

History of Litecoin

On October 7, 2011, Litecoin was released through an open-source client on GitHub by Charlie Lee, a Google employee, and later became Engineering Director at Coinbase. On October 13, 2011, the Litecoin network went live. It was a source code fork of Bitcoin Core client, varying primarily by having an increased maximum number of coins, decreased block creation time (2.5 minutes), different hashing algorithm (scrypt, rather than SHA-256) a bit modified GUI.

In November 2013, the accumulated value of Litecoin got massive growth which included within 24 hours a 100% leap.

In May 2017, Litecoin became by market cap the first top 5 cryptocurrencies to adopt isolated witness. In May, the same year through Litecoin, the first Lightning Network transaction was completed, from Zürich to San Francisco, transferring 0.00000001 LTC only in one second.

Rise of Litecoin

Litecoin gets more value than Bitcoin and is frequently referred to as digital silver to Bitcoin's digital gold statement. Both assets have a round-off supply that gives the assets a shortage aspect similar to precious metals. Litecoin cryptocurrency was grown up by more than 140% in 2020. In 2021, until May, LTC exhibited very fast growth; but, the situation significantly changed due to external factors.

From 2023-2027 five years Litecoin prediction, some believe this cryptocurrency would own a significant increase: Litecoin price would increase from $196 to $536, which is grown by 173%. As 2023 starts, Litecoin will start at $196, then within the first half of the year rise to $240 and finish that year at $283. That means from today, a total 103% increase.

Ripple
What is Ripple?

Ripple is a remittance network and currency exchange created by Ripple Labs Inc., a US-based technology company. Released in 2012, Ripple is developed upon a distributed open-source protocol and assists tokens representing cryptocurrency, fiat currency, commodities, or other units of value such as mobile minutes or frequent flier miles. Ripple claims to enable no chargebacks, secure, nearly, and instantly free global financial transactions of any size. The ledger utilizes the native cryptocurrency known as Ripple (XRP).

History of Ripple

Ripple was originated by Jed McCaleb and construct by David Schwartz and Arthur Britto, who then contact Ryan Fugger, who had launched in 2005 as a financial service to offer secure payment choices via a global network to the members of an online community. Fugger had introduced a system called OpenCoin that would transform into Ripple. The company also introduced its form of the digital currency known as XRP to offer financial institutions minor fees and wait-time to transfer money. In 2013, the company from banks reported interest in using its payment system.

By 2018, about 100 banks had signed up, but most of them only using the XCurrent messaging technology of Ripple and avoiding, due to its volatility problems, the XRP cryptocurrency. Members of the Society for Worldwide Interbank Financial Telecommunication (SWIFT), market influence is being challenged by Ripple, have contended that the scalability matters of Ripple and other blockchain solutions are not solved, limiting them to intra-bank and bilateral applications. In 2018 a Ripple executive acknowledged that "We started with your outstanding blockchain, that we love. But the feedback from banks is that you can't place the whole world on a blockchain."

Ripple depends on a common shared ledger about all Ripple accounts and a distributed database storing information. Chris Larsen explained to the Stanford Graduate School of Business that a network of independent servers administered the whole network. They compare their transaction records, and that server could belong to anyone, including market makers or banks. Ripple validates balances and accounts instantly for transfer payments and sends payment notifications within a few seconds. Payments are irreversible, and also there are no chargebacks.

As the primary contributors of code, Ripple Labs carries on the consensus verification system in the back of Ripple. In 2014, the consensus gained access to the U.S. banking system among concerns over security and a deficiency of regulation

The rise of Ripple

Cryptocurrency XRP is the digital token generated by Ripple, has seen its share price rise of late - outperforming competitors Bitcoin and Ethereum in 2021.

Within the last week, the price of XRP has doubled, from on April 7 $0.89 per share to on April 13 $1.62 per share, increasing interest attracting from investors.

Market experts believe that concluding is due to an ongoing investigation by the United States's Securities and Exchange Commission (SEC). The SEC declared that Ripple executives offering XRP through unregistered digital-asset securities increases more than $1.3 billion.

The future of Ripple

Ripple mostly stayed on the sidelines of recent price rise in cryptocurrencies, including life today, by setting down a price increase of as much as 84% percent to $0.51. As a payment network, the cryptocurrency doubles and has seen its price increases by approximately 7,500% as of this year. Its market capitalization has risen to $17 billion, from $237 million at the start of this year.

Ripple's join flock of cryptocurrencies, such as ethereum and litecoin, racked massive gains and pushed the market capitalization.

The cryptocurrency Ripple experienced a similar rise in May when its price in less than ten days tripled from $0.13 to $0.39. That price push occurred during an increase in cryptocurrency valuations across the board. After that, however, Ripple's price fluctuations until today mostly showed small increments.

The impressive development of both the cryptocurrency and Ripple technology should give traders and investors optimism. Ripple has managed to develop in a comparatively high volatility market, meaning it can resist pressure. Any progress that makes to Ripple should increase its value. Ripple itself is full of technology, finance, and Fintech experts. They believe that by concentrating on developing and acquiring partnerships and attaining customer acquisition, they can find success in arising technologies.

Stellar

What Is Stellar?

The term Stellar refers to a virtual or digital cryptocurrency created by Stellar Development Foundation. The organization's currency, which is called the lumen, is traded with the symbol XLM on various crypto exchanges. Traders can use lumens on the Stellar network based on a blockchain distributed ledger network that connects payments systems, banks, and people to offer them cross-asset transfers of value, low-cost, including payments.

Stellar, or Stellar Lumens, is a decentralized, open-source protocol for digital currency to fiat currency low-cost transfers which permit cross-border transactions between any pair of currencies. The Stellar protocol is backed by the Stellar Development Foundation, a Delaware nonprofit corporation. However, this organization does not enjoy tax-exempt 501(c)(3) status with the IRS.

History of Stellar

Stellar is operated by a nonprofit organization founded by Jed McCaleb, the Stellar Development Foundation. The Stellar project gains initial funding from the payments startup Stripe and contributions from organizations like Google, FastForward, and BlackRock. The organization accepting tax-deductible public donations offset its operational costs.

In 2018, Stellar with TransferTo signed a deal for cross-border payments to about more than 70 nations. It also obtains a Shariah-compliance certificate for asset and payments tokenization, became the first distributed technology ledger. For a double-pegged stablecoin project, Stellar was selected as a partner by IBM (IBM).

Future of Stellar

Stellar's key focus is on developing savings in bank loans and remittances to that outside of the extent of the banking services. Stellar doesn't charge institutions or individuals for using the network.

Stellar encourage a distributed exchange mode. Facilitates users to send payments in some specific currencies regardless they may hold credits in another, while the network automatically executes the forex conversion. Through a partner institute like a bank, the receiver can withdraw their currency equivalent.

Stellar aims to remarkably reduce transaction costs and time delays as a payment system that connects financial entities and cross-border transfers. While Stellar works just like Bitcoin, its basic distinguishing feature is its consensus protocol. The present-day Stellar results from a 2014 split that turns out the Stellar Consensus Protocol (SCP), following which Stellar became an open-source system. Under this protocol, the transaction authentication process is limited to a select set of authentic nodes rather than vulnerable to the whole network of nodes.

Every node on the network selects a set of authentic nodes, and a transaction is considered accepted once when authenticated by all nodes that are part of this selected group. This shortened approval cycle permits the Stellar network to keep transaction costs lower and the process of transactions faster.

Conclusion

The book "The Basics of Bitcoin and Cryptocurrency" is a very timely reference source on the emerging phenomenon of digital currencies, especially in these times of astonishing growth in public attention and popularity to cryptocurrencies. Before discussing cryptocurrencies, we should focus on the functions and value of money in our present life. Money is everything that functions as a universally excepted medium of exchange or means of payment.

When asked

"What is money?" most people respond quite reasonably that money is used to buy something—money used as a medium of exchange, which is, of course, the most familiar use. If pressed further, most would also say that money can hold as a store of value.

Money as a medium of exchange – enables people to exchange goods and services for other commodities. At home, money decreases in value because of inflation, so it is better to deposit financial assets with a bank. It can also store money in other forms like securities, bonds, or shares. We can also invest in lands, properties, arts, and jewelry.

Cryptocurrencies are hot topics in the global financial system. Money is the most valuable and in-demand commodity globally, influencing people in every aspect of their life. One of the most arguable innovations in this field is cryptocurrencies. It is a currency that is not protected by governmental regulations or law, impervious to government interference. The currency is fully decentralized, and unlike fiat money, the government cannot affect its value. The first cryptocurrency generated and the most widely used is Bitcoin. There is the high volatility of cryptocurrency exchange rates. The reason is the high risk of trading these cryptocurrencies.

Since the launch of Bitcoin in 2009, several hundred different 'cryptocurrencies' have been developed and become accepted for a wide variety of transactions in leading online commercial marketplaces and the 'sharing economy, as well as by more traditional retailers, manufacturers, and even by charities and political parties. Blockchain technology is revolutionary. It makes life safer and more superficial, changing how personal information is stored and how transactions for goods and services are produced.

Bitcoin is an electronic monetary unit and therefore has no physical representation. A Bitcoin unit can be divided into 100 million "Satoshis," which are the smallest fraction of a Bitcoin.

The Blockchain of Bitcoin is a data file that records all past Bitcoin transactions, including creating new Bitcoin units.

Blockchain technology produces a permanent and immutable record of each transaction. This inaccessible digital ledger makes fraud, data theft, hacking, and information loss impossible. The technology will affect every industry globally, including manufacturing, retail, healthcare, transportation, and real estate. Companies as Google, Microsoft, IBM, American Express, Nestle, Walmart, Chase, Intel, Dole, and Hitachi are all working to become earlier adopters of blockchain. Nearly $400 trillion across many industries is set to be transformed by blockchain.

This book has shown that blockchain technology's many features and concepts might be broadly extensible to various situations. These features did not apply just to the immediate context of currency and payments or property, contracts, and all financial markets transactions. But above to segments as diverse as government, science, literacy, health, publishing, economic development, art, and culture, and possibly even more broadly to enable orders-of-magnitude larger-scale human progress.

Blockchain technology could be quite complementary in possible space for the future world, including centralized and decentralized models. Similar to any new technology, the blockchain is an idea that initially disrupts. Over time, it could promote a larger ecosystem that includes both the old way and the innovation. Some historical examples are that the advent of the radio led to increased record sales, and e-readers such as the Kindle have increased book sales. We consume media from both large entertainment companies and YouTube. Thus, blockchain technology could exist in a larger ecosystem with both centralized and decentralized models over time.

As it stands, Bitcoin is unlikely to catch on as an official currency for the general public as it has too many faults and has too many risks. In contrast, its strengths are necessarily not something that the general public desires in an established currency. For innovation in currency to be successful, it needs to improve what the debit card and credit card have to offer.

However, it can still apply the technologies and innovation found within Bitcoin and the cryptocurrency to other technology and innovations, such as the mobile-based payment market that Apple has entered.

The technologies that come with Bitcoin have many mainstream applications. It will be fascinating to see the future technological innovations in currency and payment systems. Although Bitcoin will most likely not be a broadly popular established currency in the future, its technology will undoubtedly have widespread future implications.

Thank you, for buying the book. Hope this book helped you enriching your knowledge.

CPSIA information can be obtained
at www.ICGtesting.com
Printed in the USA
BVHW051334201221
624502BV00007B/247